Carrie Hall Blocks

Over 800 Historical Patterns

from the collection of the
Spencer Museum of Art, University of Kansas

Bettina Havig

American Quilter's Society
PO Box 3290
Paducah, KY 42002-3290

Located in Paducah, Kentucky, the American Quilter's Society (AQS) is dedicated to promoting the accomplishments of today's quilters. Through its publications and events, AQS strives to honor today's quiltmakers and their work and to inspire future creativity and innovation in quiltmaking.

Editor:	Barbara Smith
Book Design/Illustrations:	AQS Editorial Staff
Cover Design:	AQS Editorial Staff
Photography:	Clay Kappelman, unless otherwise noted.

Library of Congress Cataloging-in-Publication Data

Havig, Bettina
    Carrie Hall Blocks: over 800 historical patterns / Bettina Havig
        p.   cm.
    ISBN 0-574-32701-1
    1. Patchwork Patterns.
    2. Hall, Carrie A., b. 1866. I. Hall, Carrie A., b. 1866. II. Title
TT835.H348   1999
746.46'041--dc21   99-29390
                        CIP

Additional copies of this book may be ordered from the American Quilter's Society, PO Box 3290, Paducah, KY 42002-3290 @ $34.95. Add $2.00 for postage and handling.

ACKNOWLEDGMENTS

Thank you...

Marianne Fons and Liz Porter,
who first proposed this project;

the staff of the Spencer Museum of Art,
University of Kansas, Lawrence, Kansas:
Janet Dreiling, Nancy Corwin, and Susan Earle;

Joyce Gross, Cuesta Benberry, and Barbara Brackman
for helping me in researching Carrie Hall;

my friends Edith Leeper and Daphne Hedges,
who endured the days of sorting through blocks in the museum;

and my husband, Alan,
who always graciously endures, supports,
and encourages my quilt activities.

Contents

ABOUT THIS BOOK

*M*ore than 800 blocks are pictured in full color, accompanied by the name or names by which Carrie Hall knew them. Each block was made between 1900 and 1935. As such, they form a basis for helping to date quilts made during that period. The drafted size of each block is given along with its accession number, assigned by the Spencer Museum when the collection was given to them in 1938.

The Gallery section contains more than 600 blocks in full color, including their names, accession numbers, and sizes.

There are full-size patterns for more than 200 of the blocks. Some of the patterns were resized to fit a more appropriate grid. For example, a Nine Patch block whose original size was 10" may have been redrafted to 9" or 12". For the patterned blocks, original sizes of Carrie Hall's blocks are given in parentheses.

A block-piecing diagram accompanies each patterned block, along with a shaded diagram, showing the distribution of values in the block.

No grain lines are marked on the patterns, so please exercise good quiltmaking principles for placing the patterns so the grain falls on the outer edges of the block whenever possible. The patterns are printed with both seam lines and cutting lines to facilitate either hand or machine piecing.

Templates made from the patterns should be used face down on the wrong side of the fabric. If a pattern is marked with an *r*, such as *T12r*, then make a reverse (mirror image) of the pattern piece by laying the template face up on the wrong side of the fabric.

Many of the template patterns are used in several different blocks. If you want to make several of the block designs, you may want to create a master set of reusable templates.

Carrie Hall

*photo use provided by
Kansas State Historical Society*

Carrie Alma Hackett Hall was born December 9, 1866, in Caledonia, Wisconsin. In 1873, she moved with her family to Smith County, Kansas, where her father, Dwight Hackett, started a homestead. Though she had no secondary or college education, she did teach school for a few years in Smith County, Kansas. She was twice married, first to a man named Patterson, who shortly died of tuberculosis. Following several years of widowhood, she married John Hall, a man some years her junior.

Madame Hall, as she liked to be called, was a woman who made her own way in the world. In the early 1900s, she operated a dressmaking business, catering to the wealthy and influential women of Leavenworth, Kansas, which was, at that time, quite a cosmopolitan city. She observed the fashions and trends of her day and took the greatest advantages of her opportunities. Her dressmaking business prospered in the face of serious competition, and she employed a number of assistants and apprentices in the enterprise. All evidence supports the fact that she was a skilled needle-woman.

In the 1920s, as the demand for fancy dressmaker gowns declined, severely affecting her business, she began to look for other avenues. She noticed the vitality of the quiltmaking revival. At first, she made quilts as "pick-up" work, and later, more ardently, she began to piece blocks. Initially, she was determined to piece a cloth block for every known patchwork pattern. Madame Hall collected patterns from every possible resource and set about her goal. It was a daunting task, but she was aided by her many friends who helped to locate or design patterns. The aid of helpers is reflected in the collection of Carrie Hall block patterns at the Spencer Museum. More than 40 names of friends appear on the envelopes that contain the original pattern pieces. Perhaps some of these ladies even contributed blocks. More than 850 blocks resulted from the effort.

Madame Hall began to display the blocks and to offer programs in which she expounded on the blocks, quiltmaking, and quilt history. She apparently always appeared in colonial costume for the formal programs. In 1935, Madame Hall in collaboration with Rose Kretsinger published *The Romance of the Patchwork Quilt in America*. She organized and categorized the blocks she had produced for the publication, making it a reliable and useful resource for pattern identification. The blocks were pictured several to a page in a collage, page after page, with notes about the names of the blocks. Unfortunately, the blocks were shown only in black and white photography. (At last, in this volume, the reader can enjoy the blocks in full color.)

The Romance of the Patchwork Quilt in America quickly became a reference for quiltmakers. Her contribution to standardizing quilt pattern nomenclature is perhaps her greatest gift. The book remained the standard right into the modern quiltmaking revival. It was an absolute must to own then, and a wonderfully nostalgic book now. If you have not read it, you will find that it is both a source of information and an interesting perspective on the quiltmaking revival of the 1920s and 1930s.

Some of Madame Hall's comments underscore the universal complaint that the next generation is losing sight of what is important. "In the ready-cut quilts offered for sale are seen the effects of this hurrying age in which we live. This is especially distressing to the 'true quilter' for, as Aunt Jane of Kentucky says: 'There is a heap of comfort in making quilts, just to sit and sort over the pieces and call to mind that this piece of that is of the dress of a loved friend.' How can the modern quiltmaker know any of that joy if she must go to the store and buy her patches, an eighth of a yard here and another there – or buy a ready-cut quilt?"[1]

When interest in the blocks began to wane, she determined to give the blocks to the Thayer Museum at the University of

*photo use provided by
Kansas State Historical Society*

Kansas. The gift was made in 1938, thus the "38" in all the acquisition numbers on the blocks. The Thayer Museum was the precursor to the current Spencer Museum, which now houses the block collection.

Madame Hall continued to rely on her needle skills and her interest in fashion by publishing a second book, *From Hoopskirts to Nudity*, Caxton Printers, 1938. In 1941, at the age of 75, she moved to North Platte, Nebraska, to begin yet another career as a doll maker, doing business as The Handicraft Shop. She produced character dolls of important historic figures. She was quite successful at this enterprise.

Carrie Alma Hackett Patterson Hall died in North Platte, Nebraska, July 8, 1955. She was buried in Smith County, Kansas. Many of her scrapbooks and collections of books on various topics were acquired by St. Mary's College in Leavenworth, Kansas.[2]

In an advertisement for her books, reviewers of *The Romance of the Patchwork Quilt in America* said, "Antiques: 'This book fills a long-felt need for a concise catalogue (sic) of quilt patterns.' Hobby Rider's Guide: 'So varied a collection of designs that few who come to it will fail to find the inspiration they have sought.'"[3]

1. *The Romance of the Patchwork Quilt in America*, Hall and Kretsinger, Caxton Printers, 1935.
2. *Leavenworth Chronicle*, May 1, 1941.
3. Joyce Gross collection.

A Patchwork Quilt

Of all the things a woman's hands have made,
The quilt so lightly thrown across her bed –
The quilt that keeps her loved ones warm –
Is woven of her love and dreams and thread.

When I have spoken to you of its beauty –
"A mere hodge-podge of calico," you said,
"A necessity of homely fashioning,
Just a covering made of cloth and thread."

I knew you'd missed the message hidden there
By hands that fashioned quilts so long ago.
Ambition and assurance are the patches
And the stitches of a quilt are love, I know.

I think a quilt is something very real –
A message of creation wrought in flame;
With grief and laughter sewn into its patches
I see beyond the shadows, dream and aim.

Carrie A. Hall

First published in *The Romance of the Patchwork Quilt in America*, p. 139.

Untitled

My neighbor is washing her windows,
And scrubbing and mopping her floors,
But my house is all topsy and turvy,
And dust is behind all the doors.

My neighbor, she keeps her house spotless,
And she goes all day on a trot:
But no one would know in a fortnight
If she swept today or not.

The task I am at is enticing –
My neighbor is worn to a rag –
I am making a quilt out of pieces
I saved in a pretty chintz bag.

And the quilt, I know my descendants
Will exhibit with credit to me –
"So lovely – my grandmother made it
Long ago in 1933."

But will her grandchildren remember
Her struggles with dirt and decay?
They will not – they will wish she had made them
The quilt I am making today.

Cynicky Phin

Clipping from newspaper found on p.99, column 3 "Patchwork
Quilts" (Scrapbook #1) Carrie Hall Collection, Spencer Museum,
Lawrence, KS.

Gallery of Blocks

4 Patch

Accession: 38.415
Original Size: 8.25"

4 Patch Variation

Accession: 38.358
Original: 10.25"

4 Points

Accession: 38.32
Original Size: 11.25"

9 Patch

Accession: 38.664
Original Size: 8.25"

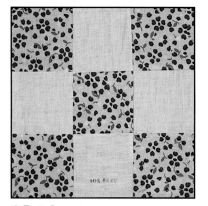

9 Patch

Accession: 38.201
Original Size: 8.25"

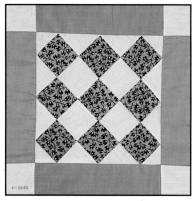

9 Patch

Accession: 38.113
Original size   13"

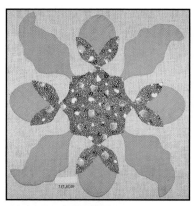

9 Patch Variation

Accession: 38.351
Original Size: 14.25"

Acorn and Oak Leaf

Accession: 38.552
Original Size: 15.5"

Airplane

Accession: 38.607
Original Size: 9.5"

Airplane
Aircraft

Accession: 38.642
Original Size: 8.5"

Airport

Accession: 38.611
Original Size: 12"

Anna Bauersfield Tulip

Accession: 38.569
Original Size: 11"

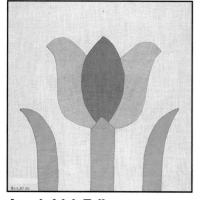

Anna's Irish Tulip

Accession: 38.568
Original Size: 12"

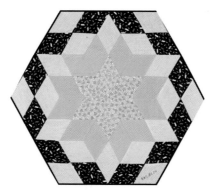

Arabian Star
Dutch Tile

Accession: 38.283
Original Size: 13.5" x 15.5"

Around the World

Accession: 38.782
Original Size: 11.5"

Aunt Eliza's Star

Accession: 38.204
Original Size: 9"

Autumn Flowers

Accession: 38.824
Original Size: 11.75" x 12"

Autumn's Tints

Accession: 38.193
Original Size: 9"

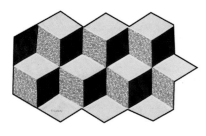

Baby Blocks

Accession: 38.235
Original Size: 10.75" x 18"

Baby Bunting

Accession: 38.85
Original Size: 10"

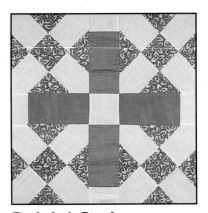

Bachelor's Puzzle

Accession: 38.472
Original Size: 14.5"

Bachelor's Puzzle

Accession: 38.399
Original Size: 13.5"

Baseball

Accession: 38.155
Original Size: 10"

Basket of Daisies

Accession: 38.756
Original Size: 12.25"

Basket of Flowers

Accession: 38.533
Original size: 13.25"

Basket of Oranges

Accession: 38.590
Original Size: 10.25"

Basket of Tulips
Basket of Lilies

Accession: 38.169
Original Size: 15.5"

Bat's Wings

Accession: 38.107
Original Size: 6" x 7.5"

Bay Leaf

Accession: 38.528
Original Size: 15.25"

Beggar's Block
Cats and Mice

Accession: 38.355
Original Size: 7.5"

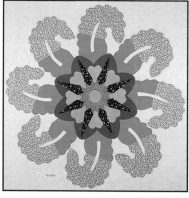

Ben Hur's Chariot Wheel

Accession: 38.523
Original Size: 25"

Big Dipper

Accession: 38.28
Original Size: 10.5"

Biloxi

Accession: 38.580
Original Size: 8.5"

Biloxi

Accession: 38.261
Original Size: 8.5"

Bird of Paradise

Accession: 38.825
Original size: 17"

Bleeding Heart

Accession: 38.56
Original Size: 11.75"

Blue Birds

Accession: 38.293
Original Size: 10.75" x 12"

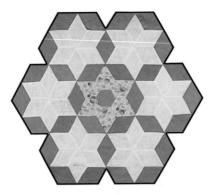

Boutonniere

Accession: 38.58
Original Size: 14" x 16"

Bow Knot
Farmer's Puzzle

Accession: 38.668
Original Size: 13"

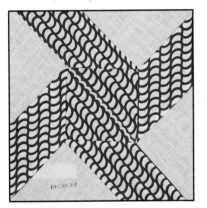

Box Quilt

Accession: 38.314
Original Size: 6"

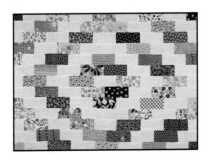

Bread Basket

Accession: 38.494
Original Size: 10.25"

Brick Pile

Accession: 38.300
Original Size: 8" x 15"

Brick Wall

Accession: 38.700
Original Size: 5.25" x 10"

Brickwork

Accession: 38.490
Original Size: 13.75" x 18"

Bridal Stairway

Accession: 38.295
Original Size: 15.25" x 27"

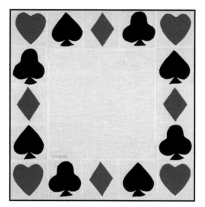

Bridge Patch

Accession: 38.554
Original Size: 15.75"

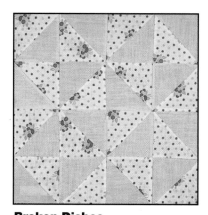

Broken Dishes

Accession: 38.34
Original Size: 11.25"

Burnham Square

Accession: 38.43
Original Size: 12.5"

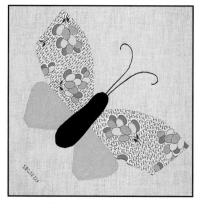

Butterfly

Accession: 38.582
Original Size: 10"

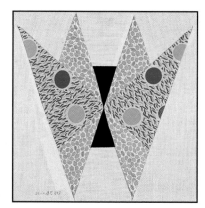

Butterfly

Accession: 38.402
Original Size: 8.25"

Butterfly

Accession: 38.586
Original Size: 9.5"

Cactus Basket
Desert Rose

Accession: 38.256
Original Size: 8"

Cactus Flower

Accession: 38.310
Original Size: 6.25"

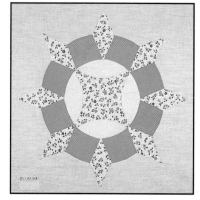

Caesar's Crown

Accession: 38.728
Original Size: 14.25"

Calico Puzzle

Accession:	38.223
Original Size:	6"

California Star

Accession:	38.247
Original Size:	29"

Capital T

Accession:	38.438
Original Size:	9.5"

Cardinal Points

Accession:	38.768
Original Size:	9"

Carlie Sexton's Flower Basket

Accession:	38.755
Original Size:	10.5"

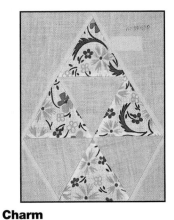

Caroline's Fan

Accession:	38.539
Original Size:	12.5"

Carpenter's Square

Accession:	38.274
Original Size:	14"

Ceremonial Plaza

Accession:	38.771
Original Size:	8.5"

Charm

Accession:	38.416
Original Size:	5.5" x 6.75"

Charter Oak

Accession: 38.598
Original Size: 13"

Cherry

Accession: 38.752
Original Size: 16"

Cherry Basket

Accession: 38.87
Original Size: 11.5"

Children of Israel

Accession: 38.330
Original Size: 9.5"

Children's Delight

Accession: 38.200
Original Size: 6.5"

Chimney Swallows

Accession: 38.620
Original Size: 13.75"

Chimney Swallows

Accession: 38.673
Original Size: 16.5"

Chimney Sweep

Accession: 38.663
Original Size: 11"

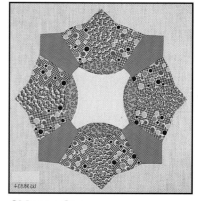

Chinese Star

Accession: 38.834
Original Size: 11"

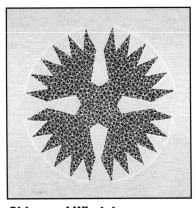

Chips and Whetstones

Accession: 38.622
Original Size: 16"

Chips and Whetstones

Accession: 38.246
Original Size: 12"

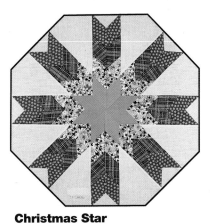

Christmas Star

Accession: 38.792
Original Size: 17.75"

Christmas Tree
Tree of Life

Accession: 38.263
Original Size: 16.75"

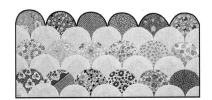

Church Steps
Log Cabin Variation

Accession: 38.292
Original Size: 10"

Churn Dasher

Accession: 38.667
Original Size: 8.25"

Circular Saw

Accession: 38.238
Original Size: 12"

Clamshell

Accession: 38.302
Original Size: 9.5" x 21"

Cleveland Tulip

Accession: 38.440
Original Size: 13.75"

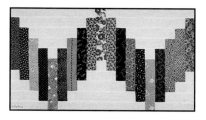

Coarse Woven

Accession: 38.273
Original Size: 12.5" x 23"

Coffee Cup

Accession: 38.610
Original Size: 7"

Cog Wheels

Accession: 38.529
Original Size: 16.25"

Colonial Basket

Accession: 38.121
Original Size: 11.5" x 12"

Colonial Tulip

Accession: 38.506
Original Size: 17.25"

Columbia Puzzle

Accession: 38.352
Original Size: 14"

Combination Rose

California Rose, Yellow Rose of Texas

Accession: 38.741
Original Size: 13"

Compass

Accession: 38.142
Original Size: 9"

Conventional Rose

Accession: 38.813
Original Size: 20.25"

Conventional Tulip

Accession: 38.740
Original Size: 13"

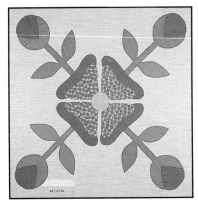

Conventional Wild Rose

Accession: 38.556
Original Size: 16"

Coronation
King's Crown

Accession: 38.683
Original Size: 11.25"

Cottage Tulips

Accession: 38.257
Original Size: 17"

Cotton Crazy Quilt

Accession: 38.78
Original Size: 15"

Courthouse Square

Accession: 38.211
Original Size: 9.5"

Cowboy's Star

Accession: 38.809
Original Size: 9.25"

Coxcomb

Accession: 38.717
Original Size: 15.5"

Coxey's Camp

Accession: 38.426
Original Size: 13.75"

Cross and Crown

Accession: 38.695
Original Size: 8.25"

Cross and Crown

Accession: 38.449
Original Size: 10"

Cross Roads

Accession: 38.133
Original Size: 13"

Cross Within a Cross

Accession: 38.793
Original Size: 10.5"

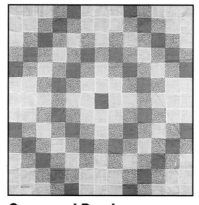

Crossword Puzzle

Accession: 38.266
Original Size: 20" x 21"

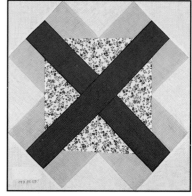

Crow's Foot

Accession: 38.430
Original Size: 12.25"

Crow's Nest

Accession: 38.350
Original Size: 12.5"

Crown of Thorns
New York Beauty
Rocky Mountain Road

Accession: 38.81
Original Size: 15.5"

Crowned Cross
Cross and Crown

Accession: 38.675
Original Size: 10.75"

Cube Work

Accession: 38.27
Original Size: 10.5" x 11"

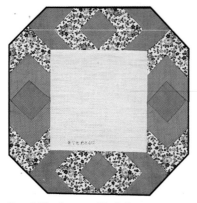

Cupid's Arrow Point

Accession: 38.373
Original Size: 8.75"

Currants and Cockscomb

Accession: 38.736
Original Size: 14"

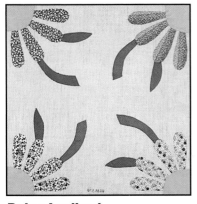

Daisy Appliqué

Accession: 38.570
Original Size: 13"

Daisy Chain

Accession: 38.592
Original Size: 17" irregular shape

David and Goliath

Accession: 38.646
Original Size: 12.75"

Democrat Donkey

Accession: 38.319
Original Size: 20" x 22.5"

Diamond and Cube

Accession: 38.160
Original Size: 11.75" x 12"

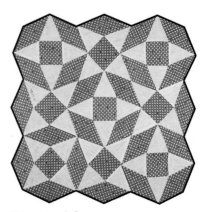

Diamond Star

Accession: 38.57
Original Size: 13"

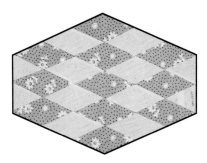

Diamonds

Accession: 38.469
Original Size: 9" x 12.25"

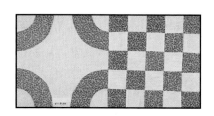

Dogwood Blossoms

Accession: 38.178
Original Size: 10" x 20"

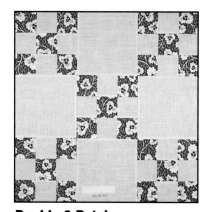

Double 9 Patch

Accession: 38.631
Original Size: 13.75"

Double 9 Patch

Accession: 38.131
Original Size: 12.25"

Double Hearts
St. Valentine's Patch

Accession: 38.816
Original Size: 10"

Double Irish Chain
Chained 5 Patch

Accession: 38.707
Original Size: 9.5" x 18.5"

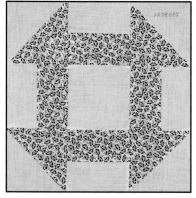

Double Monkey Wrench

Accession: 38.662
Original Size: 9"

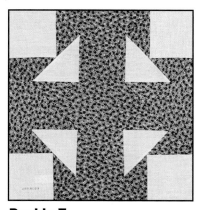

Double T

Accession: 38.445
Original Size: 12.25"

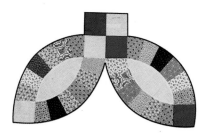

Double Wedding Ring

Accession: 38.468
Original Size: 16" x 24.5"

Double X

Accession: 38.489A
Original Size: 8.75" x 9.25"

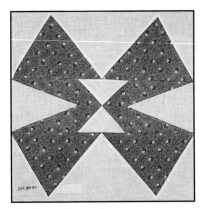

Double Z

Accession: 38.365
Original Size: 10.5"

Dove In the Window

Accession: 38.686
Original Size: 7" x 8.25"

Dove of Peace

Accession: 38.463
Original Size: 21"

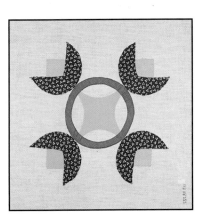

Drunkard's Path

Accession: 38.784
Original Size: 16.5"

Dusty Miller

Accession: 38.670
Original Size: 15.75"

Dutch Mill

Accession: 38.40
Original Size: 12.5"

Dutch Tulip

Accession: 38.727
Original Size: 14.25"

(Earliest Known) Rose of Sharon

Accession: 38.710
Original Size: 16"

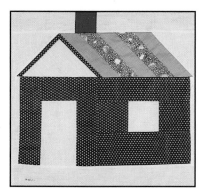

Early Colonial Cottage

| Accession: | 38.16 |
| Original Size: | 14.5" x 15" |

Easter Lily

| Accession: | 38.567 |
| Original Size: | 12.5" x 12.7" |

Eccentric Star
Churn Dasher

| Accession: | 38.192 |
| Original Size: | 7.75" |

Economy Patch

| Accession: | 38.382 |
| Original Size: | 7.5" |

Elephant Ararat

| Accession: | 38.322 |
| Original Size: | 16' x 20.75" |

English Flower Pot
English Flower Garden

| Accession: | 38.544 |
| Original Size: | 13.25" x 14" |

English Poppy

| Accession: | 38.508 |
| Original Size: | 18.75" |

English Rose

| Accession: | 38.501 |
| Original Size: | 21.5" |

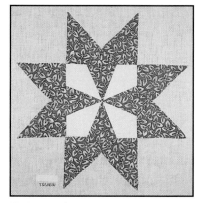

Enigma Star

| Accession: | 38.527 |
| Original Size: | 14.5" |

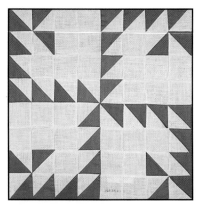

Eternal Triangle

Accession: 38.401
Original Size: 13"

Evening Star

Accession: 38.462
Original Size: 8.5"

Evening Star

Accession: 38.285
Original Size: 11.75"

Falling Timber

Accession: 38.336
Original Size: 11.5"

Fanny's Fan

Accession: 38.75
Original Size: 15"

Fanny's Favorite

Accession: 38.408
Original Size: 17.25"

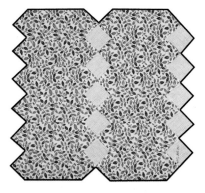

Fantastic Patchwork

Accession: 38.299
Original Size: 12" x 13.25"

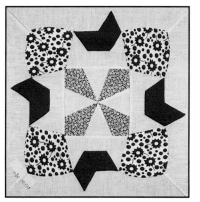

Farmer's Wife

Accession: 38.749
Original Size: 12.25"

Feather Crown with Ragged Robin in Center

Accession: 38.712
Original Size: 17.5"

**Feather Star
with Sawtooth Border**

Accession: 38.321
Original Size: 13.75" x 14"

Feather(ed) Star...
*Twinkling Star, Star of Bethlehem,
Saw Tooth, Chestnut Burr*

Accession: 38.461
Original Size: 16.25"

Fence Row

Accession: 38.281
Original Size: 9x25"

Fence Row

Accession: 38.484
Original Size: 8" x 11"

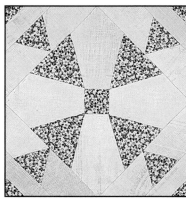

Fern

Accession: 38.763
Original Size: 11"

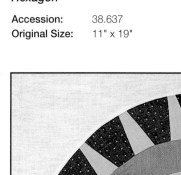

Ferris Wheel
Hexagon

Accession: 38.637
Original Size: 11" x 19"

Five (5) Point Star

Accession: 38.530
Original Size: 14.25"

Fleurs-de-lis

Accession: 38.564
Original Size: 11.5"

Flo's Fan

Accession: 38.96
Original Size: 8.5"

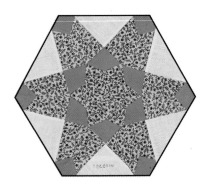

Florida Star

Accession: 38.385
Original Size: 8.75" x 10"

Flower Star

Accession: 38.819
Original Size: 13.25"

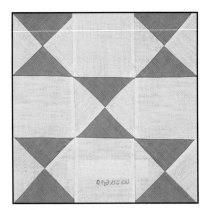

Flying X

Accession: 38.649
Original Size: 6.5"

Fool's Puzzle

Accession: 38.334
Original Size: 11.25"

Fool's Puzzle

Accession: 38.333
Original Size: 11.5"

Forbidden Fruit Tree

Accession: 38.248
Original Size: 12" x 13.25"

Formosa Tea Leaf

Accession: 38.451
Original Size: 14"

Four (4) Little Baskets

Accession: 38.122
Original Size: 14"

Four (4) Peonies

Accession: 38.540
Original Size: 15.75"

Four (4) Tulips

Accession:	38.583
Original Size:	10"

Four (4) Tulips

Accession:	38.830
Original Size:	17"

Four H Club

Accession:	38.770
Original Size:	8"

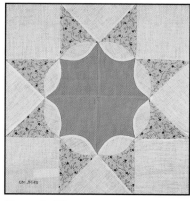

French Star

Accession:	38.163
Original Size:	11.5"

Friendship Dahlia

Accession:	38.597
Original Size:	13"

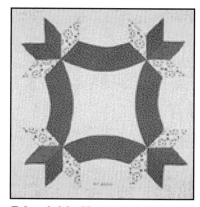

Friendship Knot

Accession:	38.715
Original Size:	13.75"

Friendship Quilt

Accession:	38.288
Original Size:	13.25"

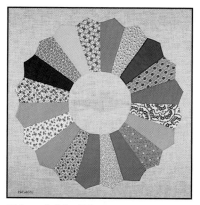

Friendship Ring
Dresden Plate, Aster

Accession:	38.549
Original Size:	16.5"

Full Blown Tulip

Accession:	38.608
Original Size:	12"

Garden Maze

Accession: 38.470
Original Size: 11.75"

Geometric Star

Accession: 38.781
Original Size: 8.5"

Georgetown Circle

Accession: 38.473
Original Size: 15.5"

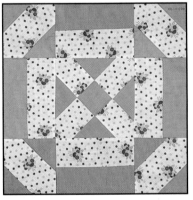

Girl's Joy

Accession: 38.409
Original Size: 12"

Goblet

Accession: 38.198
Original Size: 5.25"

Godey's Lady's Book Block

Accession: 38.181
Original Size: 12"

Golden Corn

Accession: 38.551
Original Size: 14"

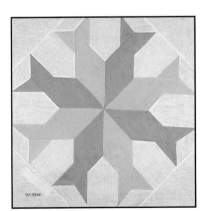

Gold Fish Block

Accession: 38.397
Original Size: 15"

Godey's Lady's Book Block

Accession: 38.475
Original Size: 11.5"

Golden Gate
Winged Square

Accession: 38.108
Original Size: 16.5"

Golden Glow

Accession: 38.395
Original Size: 11.5"

Golden Glow

Accession: 38.471
Original Size: 18.75"

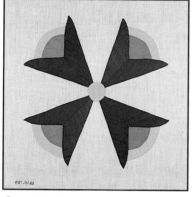

Grandma's Tulips

Accession: 38.758
Original Size: 12.25"

Grandmother's Basket

Accession: 38.22
Original Size: 10"

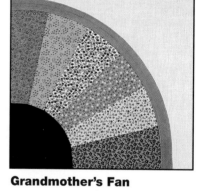

Grandmother's Fan

Accession: 38.362
Original Size: 11.75"

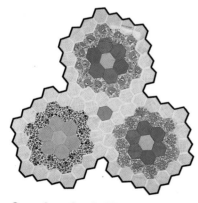

Grandmother's Flower Garden
French Bouquet

Accession: 38.308
Original Size: 8.5" each rosette

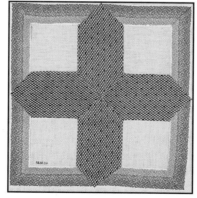

Grandmother's Own

Accession: 38.36
Original Size: 11.75"

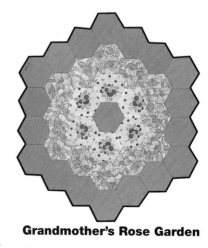

Grandmother's Rose Garden

Accession: 38.487
Original Size: 10.75" x 9.7"

Greek Cross

Accession: 38.207
Original Size: 9.5"

Harrison Rose

Accession: 38.738
Original Size: 16"

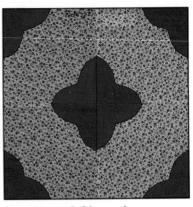

Hearts and Gizzard
Pierrot's PomPom

Accession: 38.353
Original Size: 10.25"

Hero's Crown

Accession: 38.724
Original Size: 13.25"

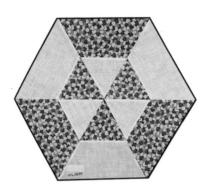

Hexagon

Accession: 38.287
Original Size: 12" x 13.75"

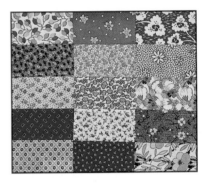

Hit or Miss
Hit and Miss

Accession: 38.467
Original Size: 8.5" x 10"

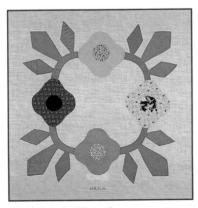

Hollyhock Wreath

Accession: 38.826
Original Size: 16"

Home Treasure

Accession: 38.423
Original Size: 10.25"

Honey Bee

Accession: 38.561
Original Size: 11.5"

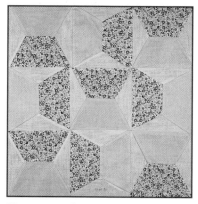

Honeycomb

Accession:	38.55
Original Size:	12.25" x 12"

Honeycomb

Accession:	38.161
Original Size:	11.25" x 12"

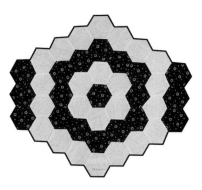

Honeycomb

Accession:	38.485
Original Size:	12.5"

Honeymoon Cottage

Accession:	38.585
Original Size:	9" x 11.5"

Horn of Plenty

Accession:	38.521
Original Size:	17.5"

Horn of Plenty

Accession:	38.601
Original Size:	11.25"

Hour Glass

Accession:	38.684
Original Size:	7.75"

Hour Glass

Accession:	38.191
Original Size:	8.25"

House that Jack Built

Accession:	38.270
Original Size:	13.5"

Hozannah or Psalm

Accession: 38.312
Original Size: 12"

Hunter's Star

Accession: 38.808
Original Size: 17"

Hyacinths

Accession: 38.836
Original Size: 18"

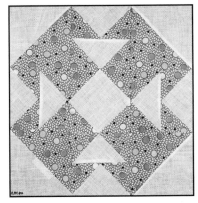

Ice Cream Bowl

Accession: 38.47
Original Size: 13"

Imperial T

Accession: 38.33
Original Size: 10.75"

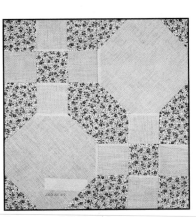

Improved 9 Patch

Accession: 38.632
Original Size: 12.25"

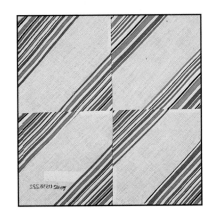

Indian Hatchet

Accession: 38.222
Original Size: 9.25"

Indian Hatchet

Accession: 38.672
Original Size: 16.5"

Indiana Rose

Accession: 38.750
Original Size: 14.5"

Inlay Star

Accession: 38.138
Original Size: 18.75"

Iowa Rose Wreath

Accession: 38.754
Original Size: 15.25"

Iris

Accession: 38.596
Original Size: 11.25"

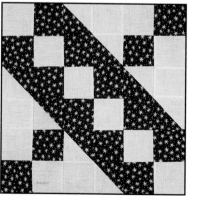

Iris

Accession: 38.547
Original Size: 13.75"

Iris

Accession: 38.572
Original Size: 12.25" x 20"

Iris Leaf
Wandering Foot

Accession: 38.573
Original Size: 14.5"

Jacob's Ladder

Accession: 38.616
Original Size: 12.5"

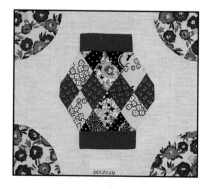

Japanese Lantern

Accession: 38.588
Original Size: 9.75"

Jewel

Accession: 38.619
Original Size: 15"

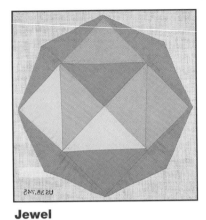

Jewel

Accession: 38.745
Original Size: 9"

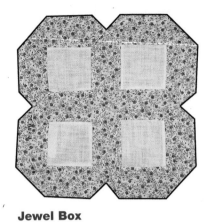

Jewel Box

Accession: 38.371
Original Size: 8.5"

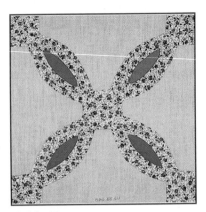

Job's Tears

Accession: 38.648
Original Size: 9.75"

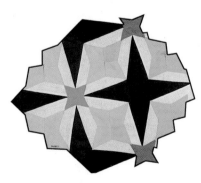

Kaleidoscope

Accession: 38.414
Original Size: 6"

Kaleidoscope

Accession: 38.286
Original Size: 12.25"

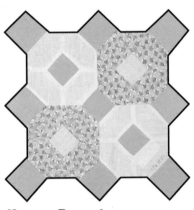

Kansas Dugout

Accession: 38.635
Original Size: 12.75"

Kansas Star

Accession: 38.605
Original Size: 14" x 17"

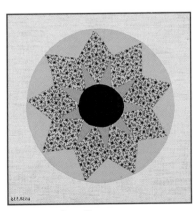

Kansas Sunflower

Accession: 38.536
Original Size: 13"

KC Star Exhibition Home

Accession: 38.364
Original Size: 11.75" x 12"

Bettina Havig

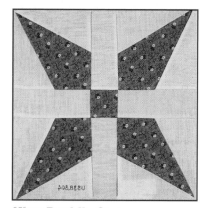

King David's Crown

Accession: 38.647
Original Size: 11"

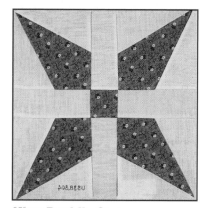

King David's Crown

Accession: 38.804
Original Size: 8.75"

King's Crown

Accession: 38.203
Original Size: 8.5"

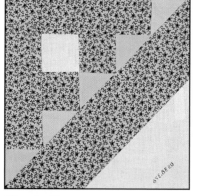

King's Crown

Accession: 38.376
Original Size: 9"

King's Star

Accession: 38.800
Original Size: 11.25"

Kitty Corner

Accession: 38.651
Original Size: 12.25"

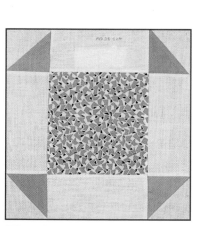

Kitty Corner
Puss in the Corner

Accession: 38.456
Original Size: 7.75"

L Stripe

Accession: 38.176
Original Size: 12.75"

Lady Fingers
Sunflowers

Accession: 38.510
Original Size: 17.75"

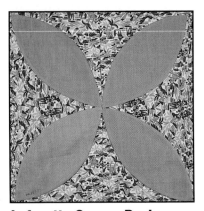

Lafayette Orange Peel

Accession: 38.44
Original Size: 11"

Lattice

Accession: 38.343
Original Size: 16.5"

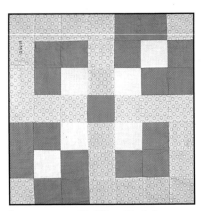

Leavenworth Nine Patch

Accession: 38.61
Original Size: 12.5"

Leavenworth Star

Accession: 38.307
Original Size: 13"

Letter A

Accession: 38.413
Original Size: 12"

Letter E

Accession: 38.294
Original Size: 18"

Letter H

Accession: 38.209
Original Size: 9"

Letter X

Accession: 38.206
Original Size: 9.25"

Letter X

Accession: 38.205
Original Size: 9"

Lily

Accession: 38.62
Original Size: 12.5"

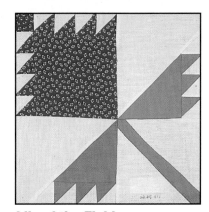

Lily of the Field

Accession: 38.80
Original Size: 9.5"

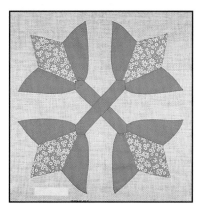

Lily of the Valley

Accession: 38.535
Original Size: 13.5"

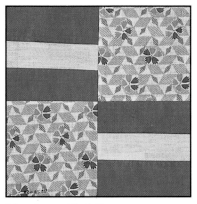

Linoleum Patch

Accession: 38.459
Original Size: 7.25"

Little Beech Tree

Accession: 38.249
Original Size: 12"

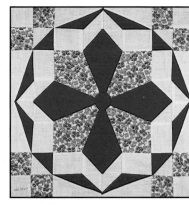

Little Giant
Heart's Desire

Accession: 38.688
Original Size: 15"

Little Sawtooth
*Lend & Borrow, Rocky Glen,
Indian Meadow, Lost Ship*

Accession: 38.239
Original Size: 11.75" x 12"

Live Oak Tree

Accession: 38.264
Original Size: 16"

Lock and Chain

Accession: 38.390
Original Size: 10.75"

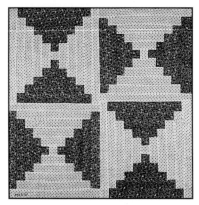

Log Cabin
Courthouse Steps

Accession: 38.644
Original Size: 17"

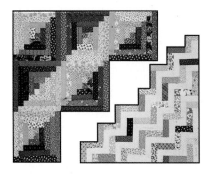

Log Cabin Barn Raising
Fine Woven Patchwork

Accession: 38.279
Original Size: 16" x 29.5"

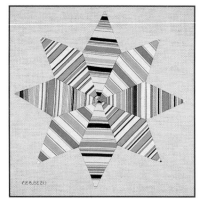

Log Cabin Star

Accession: 38.835
Original Size: 11.25"

Log Cabin Straight Furrow

Accession: 38.640
Original Size: 23"

Log Patch

Accession: 38.272
Original Size: 13.5"

London Roads

Accession: 38.110
Original Size: 12"

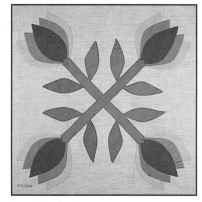

Lone Eagle

Accession: 38.609
Original Size: 12"

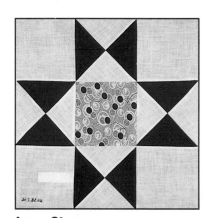

Lone Star
Texas Star

Accession: 38.214
Original Size: 12.25"

Loretta's Rose

Accession: 38.560
Original Size: 16.25"

Lotus Bud

Accession: 38.818
Original Size: 16"

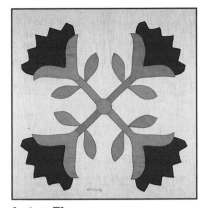

Lotus Flower

Accession: 38.719
Original Size: 16"

Love Apple

Accession: 38.718
Original Size: 14.5"

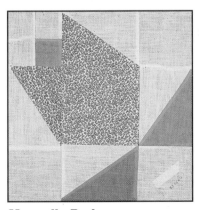

Lover's Knot

Accession: 38.557
Original Size: 12" x 17.25"

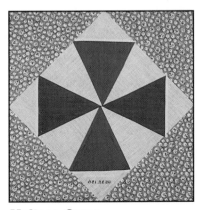

Madam X

Accession: 38.277
Original Size: 17.5"

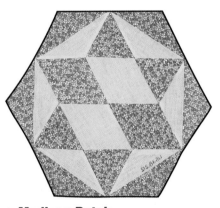

Madison Patch

Accession: 38.212
Original Size: 10.5"

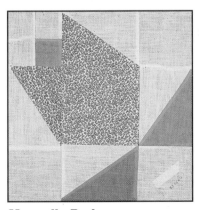

Magnolia Bud

Accession: 38.84
Original Size: 9.5"

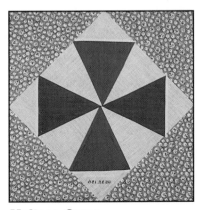

Maltese Cross

Accession: 38.156
Original Size: 10.25"

Maltese Cross
Pineapple

Accession: 38.801
Original Size: 12"

Martha Washington's Wreath

Accession: 38.746
Original Size: 16.75"

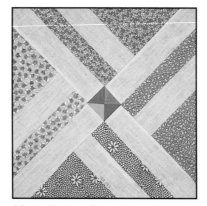

Mary Tenny Grey Travel Patch

Accession: 38.621
Original Size: 10.5"

Maud Hare's Flower Garden

Accession: 38.815
Original Size: 19"

Maude Hare's Basket

Accession: 38.751
Original Size: 16"

Meadow Daisy
Black-Eyed Susan

Accession: 38.720
Original Size: 16"

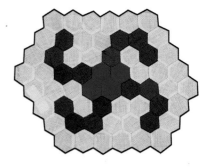

Mella Mosaic

Accession: 38.488
Original Size: 10.5"

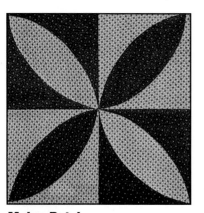

Melon Patch

Accession: 38.655
Original Size: 11.75'

Mexican Rose

Accession: 38.537
Original Size: 14"

Mexican Rose

Accession: 38.732
Original Size: 18"

Mexican Rose

Accession: 38.517
Original Size: 16.5"

Mexican Star

Accession: 38.798
Original Size: 10.5"

Milky Way

Accession: 38.175
Original Size: 15"

Mill Wheel

Accession: 38.783
Original Size: 12"

Missouri Rose
Rose Tree, Prairie Flower

Accession: 38.747
Original Size: 21.25"

Mixed T

Accession: 38.427
Original Size: 12.75"

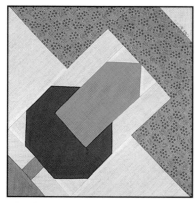

Modern Pieced Acorn

Accession: 38.190
Original Size: 9"

Modern Pieced California Poppy

Accession: 38.493
Original Size: 8.5" x 11"

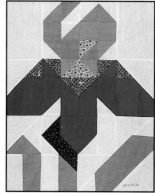

Modern Pieced Iris

Accession: 38.298
Original Size: 12" x 15"

Modern Pieced Pansy

Accession: 38.41
Original Size: 12"

Modern Pieced Rose

Accession: 38.149
Original Size: 14.25"

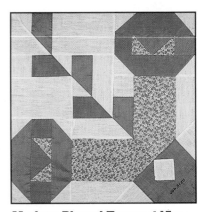

Modern Pieced Trumpet Vine

Accession: 38.400
Original Size: 13.75"

Modern Pieced Tulip

Accession: 38.38
Original Size: 9.5" x 16"

Modern Star

Accession: 38.531
Original Size: 13"

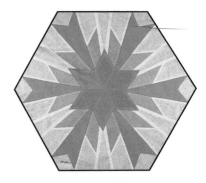

Modernistic Star

Accession: 38.251
Original Size: 20.25"

Mollie's Choice

Accession: 38.66
Original Size: 13.5"

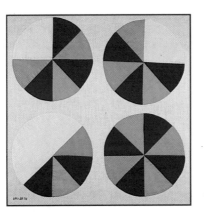

Moon and Stars

Accession: 38.496
Original Size: 17.5"

Morning Glory

Accession: 38.509
Original Size: 19"

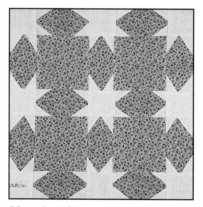

Morning Star

Accession:	38.213
Original Size:	10.75"

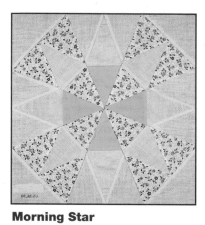

Morning Star

Accession:	38.90
Original Size:	11"

Morning Star

Accession:	38.39
Original Size:	12.75"

Mosaic #1

Accession:	38.491T
Original Size:	7"

Mosaic #2

Accession:	38.491A
Original Size:	7.25"

Mosaic #3

Accession:	38.491B
Original Size:	10"

Mosaic #4

Accession:	38.491C
Original Size:	9"

Mosaic #5

Accession:	38.491W
Original Size:	8.25"

Mosaic #6

Accession:	38.491V
Original Size:	9.75" x 10"

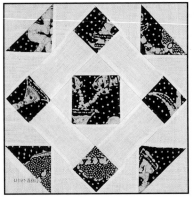

Mosaic #7

Accession: 38.491U
Original Size: 9"

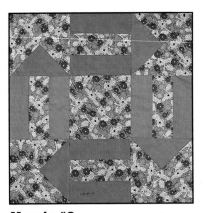

Mosaic #8

Accession: 38.491D
Original Size: 13.75"

Mosaic #9

Accession: 38.491E
Original Size: 12"

Mosaic #10

Accession: 38.491P
Original Size: 10.75"

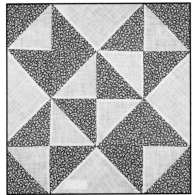

Mosaic #11

Accession: 38.491Q
Original Size: 11.5"

Mosaic #12

Accession: 38.491S
Original Size: 8.25" x 8.75"

Mosaic #13

Accession: 38.491F
Original Size: 9"

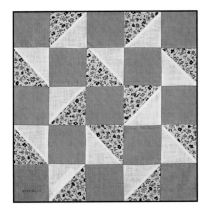

Mosaic #14

Accession: 38.491G
Original Size: 10.5"

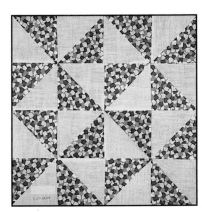

Mosaic #15

Accession: 38.491R
Original Size: 9"

Mosaic #16

Accession:	38.491H
Original Size:	8.5"

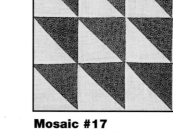

Mosaic #17

Accession:	38.491J
Original Size:	9.75"

Mosaic #18

Accession:	38.491I
Original Size:	9.5"

Mosaic #19

Accession:	38.491K
Original Size:	10.5"

Mosaic #20

Accession:	38.491L
Original Size:	12"

Mosaic #21

Accession:	38.491M
Original Size:	11"

Mosaic #22

Accession:	38.491N
Original Size:	9"

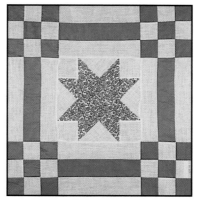

Mother's Fancy Star

Accession:	38.342
Original Size:	16.5"

Mountain Laurel

Accession:	38.504
Original Size:	28"

Mountain Pink

Accession: 38.606
Original Size: 11"

Mrs. Ever's Tulip

Accession: 38.613
Original Size: 9.5"

Mrs. Hall's Basket

Accession: 38.541
Original Size: 13.75" x 14"

Mrs. Harris' Colonial Rose

Accession: 38.839
Original Size: 17"

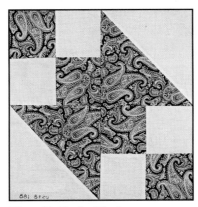

Mrs. Keller's Choice

Accession: 38.188
Original Size: 9"

Mrs. Kretsinger's Rose

Accession: 38.760
Original Size: 13.5"

Mrs. Morgan's Choice

Accession: 38.186
Original Size: 15.25"

Mystery Flower Garden

Accession: 38.258
Original Size: 5.25" x 5.5"

Navajo Squash Blossom

Accession: 38.829
Original Size: 10"

Navajo Weaving

Accession: 38.766
Original Size: 8"

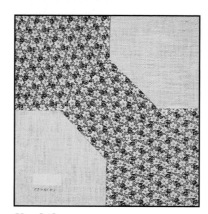

Necktie

Accession: 38.453
Original Size: 8.5"

Necktie

Accession: 38.654
Original Size: 6.25"

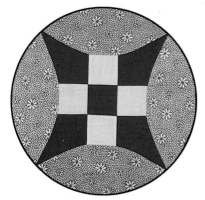

Nelson's Victory

Accession: 38.658
Original Size: 10.25"

New 4 Patch

Accession: 38.83
Original Size: 16"

New Star

Accession: 38.789
Original Size: 10"

Nine Patch

Accession: 38.618
Original Size: 11"

No Name Patch

Accession: 38.356
Original Size: 8.5"

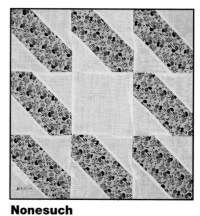

Nonesuch

Accession: 38.432
Original Size: 11"

Nonesuch

Loose Ring

Accession: 38.301
Original Size: 22.75"

Nonsense

Accession: 38.315
Original Size: 7.5"

North Carolina Lily

Accession: 38.739
Original Size: 12"

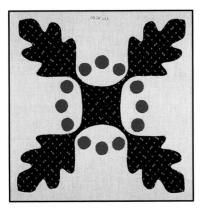

Nose Gay

Accession: 38.255
Original Size: 8"

Oak Leaf

Accession: 38.725
Original Size: 11.25"

Oak Leaf and Acorn

Accession: 38.594
Original Size: 12.75

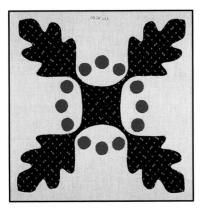

Oak Leaf and Cherries

Accession: 38.757
Original Size: 13"

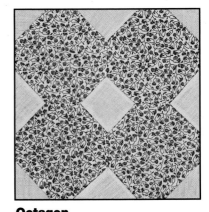

Ocean Wave

Accession: 38.241
Original Size: 18.5"

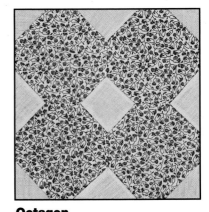

Octagon

Accession: 38.455
Original Size: 6.5"

Odd Fellow's Cross

Accession: 38.694
Original Size: 9.5"

Odd Star

Accession: 38.173
Original Size: 15"

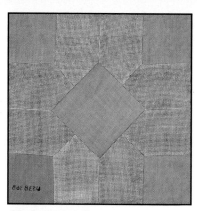

Oh Susannah

Accession: 38.368
Original Size: 9"

Ohio Rose

Accession: 38.734
Original Size: 17.5"

Ohio Rose

Accession: 38.602
Original Size: 13.75"

Ohio Rose

Accession: 38.833
Original Size: 21" x 22"

Ohio Star
*Variable Star, Lone Star, Texas
Star, Mystery Flower Garden*

Accession: 38.215
Original Size: 12.75"

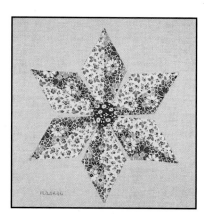

Old Colony Star

Accession: 38.831
Original Size: 11.25"

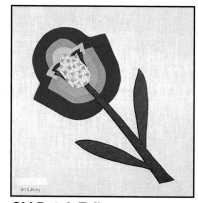

Old Dutch Tulip

Accession: 38.574
Original Size: 12"

Old Fashioned Garden Flower

Accession: 38.566
Original Size: 12" x 12.75"

Old Fashioned Nosegay

Accession: 38.559
Original Size: 16"

Old Fashioned Rose

Accession: 38.820
Original Size: 17"

Old Homestead

Accession: 38.584
Original Size: 9.25" x 12.5"

Old Tippecanoe

Accession: 38.217
Original Size: 12"

Old Tippecanoe

Accession: 38.332
Original Size: 11.5"

Oriental Poppy

Accession: 38.822
Original Size: 21.75"

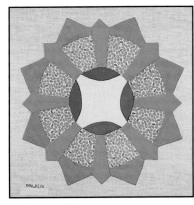

Oriental Star

Accession: 38.600
Original Size: 12.25"

Original Rose

Accession: 38.729
Original Size: 17"

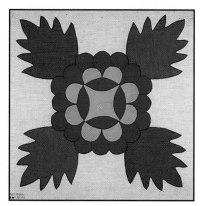

Original Rose #3

Accession: 38.761
Original Size: 15"

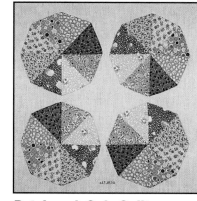

Patchwork Sofa Quilt

Accession: 38.534
Original Size: 14"

Paths to Peace

Accession: 38.112
Original Size: 13"

Patience Corners

Accession: 38.483
Original Size: 12"

Patricia's Patch

Accession: 38.614
Original Size: 7.75"

Patty's Star

Accession: 38.791
Original Size: 19.25"

Peeny Pen's Cottage

Accession: 38.555
Original Size: 12" x 13"

Peonies

Accession: 38.742
Original Size: 12.25"

Peony

Accession: 38.723
Original Size: 12.5"

Peony Patch

Accession: 38.167
Original Size: 15"x 17"

Persian Star

Accession: 38.171
Original Size: 16"

Philopena

Accession: 38.231
Original Size: 14.25"

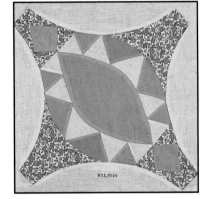

Pickle Dish

Accession: 38.228
Original Size: 11"

Pickle Dish

Accession: 38.227
Original Size: 12.75"

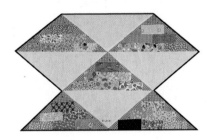

Pieced Pyramids

Accession: 38.278
Original size: 13" x 21"

Pine Tree

Accession: 38.482
Original Size: 17" x 18.5"

Pineapple

Accession: 38.743
Original Size: 9.5"

Pineapple

Accession: 38.812
Original Size: 16"

Pineapple

Accession: 38.500
Original Size: 17"

Pineapple
Maltese Cross

Accession: 38.291
Original Size: 17.5"

Pinwheel

Accession: 38.660
Original Size: 10.25"

Pinwheel
Flutter Wheel

Accession: 38.118
Original Size: 12"

Pinwheel Star

Accession: 38.435
Original Size: 14.25"

Poinsettia

Accession: 38.832
Original Size: 17"

Poinsettia

Accession: 38.503
Original Size: 16"

Poinsettia

Accession: 38.735
Original Size: 12.5"

Poinsettia
Flower of Christmas

Accession: 38.526
Original Size: 18"

Polaris Star
Flying Bat

Accession: 38.99
Original Size   13.5"

Pomegranate

Accession: 38.519
Original Size: 19.75"

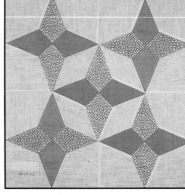

Pontiac Star

Accession: 38.46
Original Size: 11.5"

Poplar Leaf

Accession: 38.576
Original Size: 10"

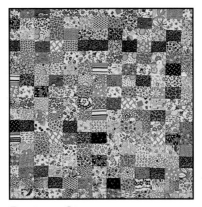

Postage Stamp

Accession: 38.410
Original Size: 12.5"

Potted Tulips

Accession: 38.518
Original Size: 26"

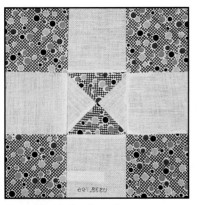

Practical Orchard

Accession: 38.796
Original Size: 8.25"

Prairie Star
Harvest Sun, Ship's Wheel

Accession: 38.687
Original Size: 17.5"

President's Quilt

Accession: 38.242
Original Size: 15"

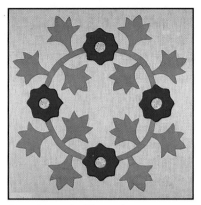

President's Wreath

Accession: 38.811
Original Size: 18.5"

Pride of the Forest

Accession: 38.711
Original Size: 18.5"

Primrose Path

Accession: 38.677
Original Size: 13.75"

Princess Feather
Star & Plumes

Accession: 38.513
Original Size: 18.25"

Puffed Silk Quilt

Accession: 38.638
Original Size: 8"

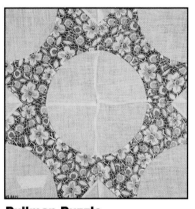

Pullman Puzzle

Accession: 38.25
Original Size: 10.75"

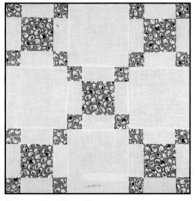

Puss-in-the-Corner

Accession: 38.625
Original Size: 14.5"

Pyrotechnics

Accession: 38.794
Original Size: 20"

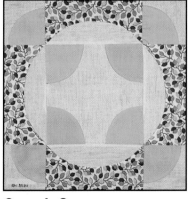

Queen's Crown

Accession: 38.145
Original Size: 11.75"

Radical Rose

Accession: 38.515
Original Size: 17"

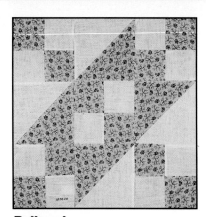

Railroad

Accession: 38.93
Original Size: 12"

Rainbow

Accession: 38.153
Original Size: 18.75" x 9.5"

Rainbow Tile

Accession: 38.253
Original Size: 15"

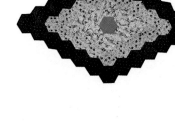

Rainbow Tile
Diamond Field

Accession: 38.636
Original Size: 11.75" x 19"

Rebecca's Fan

Accession: 38.50
Original Size: 13.5"

Red Birds

Accession: 38.603
Original Size: 11.5"

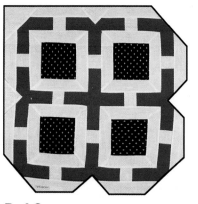

Red Cross

Accession: 38.269
Original Size: 15"

Reel (The)

Accession: 38.721
Original Size: 12"

Bettina Havig

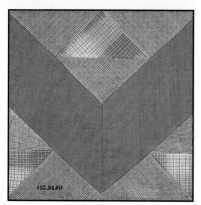

Ribbon Border Block

Accession: 38.221
Original Size: 8.75"

Rising Sun

Accession: 38.189
Original Size: 9.75"

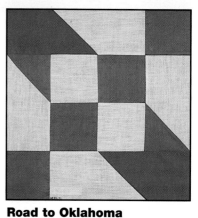

Road to Oklahoma

Accession: 38.35
Original Size: 11.5"

Robbing Peter to Pay Paul

Accession: 38.79
Original Size: 16"

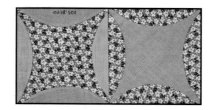

Robbing Peter to Pay Paul
Orange Peel

Accession: 38.701
Original Size: 5.5" x 10.75"

Rockingham's Beauty

Accession: 38.104
Original Size: 13"

Rocky Road to Kansas

Accession: 38.30
Original Size: 11"

Rolling Pin
Wheel

Accession: 38.74
Original Size: 15"

Roman Cross

Accession: 38.425
Original Size: 10.25"

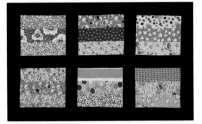

Roman Square

Accession: 38.704
Original Size: 9" x 14.25"

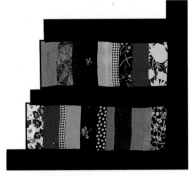

Roman Stripe

Accession: 38.639
Original Size: 13" x 15"

Rose Appliqué

Accession: 38.571
Original Size: 12"

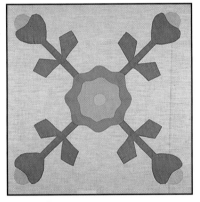

Rose Cross

Accession: 38.497
Original Size: 17.5"

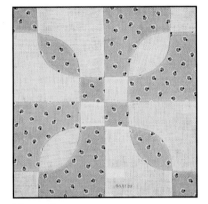

Rose Dream

Accession: 38.60
Original Size: 12.75"

Rose of LeMoyne

Accession: 38.737
Original Size: 14.5"

Rose of Sharon

Accession: 38.713
Original Size: 20.25"

Rose of Sharon

Accession: 38.514
Original Size: 17"

Rose of Sharon

Accession: 38.730
Original Size: 17"

Rose of Sharon

Accession: 38.748
Original Size: 22"

Rose of Sharon

Accession: 38.507
Original Size: 18"

Rose of Sharon

Accession: 38.558
Original Size: 16"

Rose of Sharon

Accession: 38.525
Original Size: 19"

Rose Tree

Accession: 38.511
Original Size: 17.5"

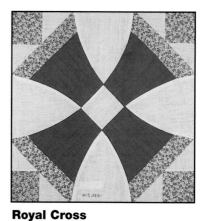

Royal Cross

Accession: 38.236
Original Size: 12"

Royal Star

Accession: 38.744
Original Size: 10.5"

Sadie's Choice Rose

Accession: 38.753
Original Size: 14"

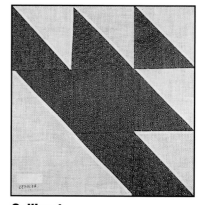

Sailboat

Accession: 38.433
Original Size: 10.75"

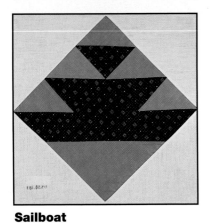

Sailboat

Accession:	38.183
Original Size:	11"

Sara's Favorite

Accession:	38.486
Original Size:	12.5"

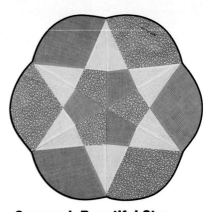

Savannah Beautiful Star

Accession:	38.786
Original Size:	13.5" x 14.7"

Sawtooth (Star)

Accession:	38.100
Original Size:	8.25"

Scotch Thistle

Accession:	38.814
Original Size:	17.25"

Semi-Octagon

Accession:	38.259
Original Size:	11"

Setting Sun

Accession:	38.593
Original Size:	14.75"

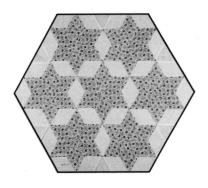

Seven Sisters
Seven Stars

Accession:	38.95
Original Size:	18" x 20.5"

Shadows

Accession:	38.265
Original Size:	6.25x9"

Shamrock

Accession:	38.589
Original Size:	8"

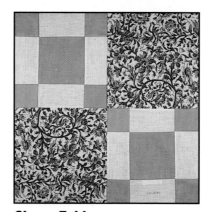

Sheep Fold

Accession:	38.340
Original Size:	16"

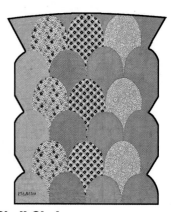

Shell Chain

Accession:	38.375
Original Size:	10" x 12.25"

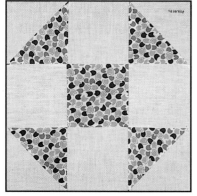

Shoo Fly

Accession:	38.184
Original Size:	12.25"

Simple Design

Accession:	38.344
Original Size:	16"

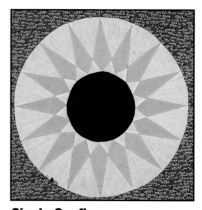

Single Sunflower

Accession:	38.18
Original Size:	11.5"

Slashed Star

Accession:	38.495
Original Size:	18"

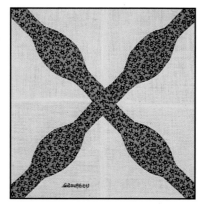

Snail's Trail

Accession:	38.579
Original Size:	8.5"

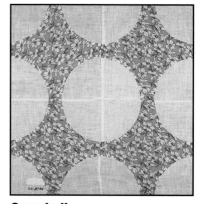

Snowball

Accession:	38.165
Original Size:	15.5"

Snowball

Accession: 38.154
Original Size: 12.25"

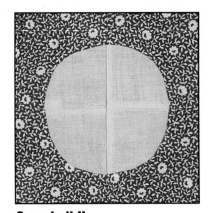

Snowball II

Accession: 38.325A
Original Size: 5"

Snowflake

Accession: 38.457
Original Size: 6.75"

Spice Pink

Accession: 38.714
Original Size: 20"

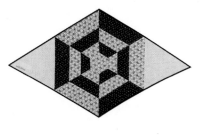

Spider Web

Accession: 38.240
Original Size: 12.5" x 22.2"

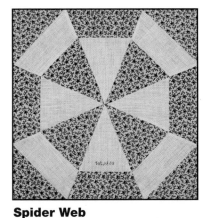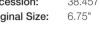

Spider Web

Accession: 38.267
Original Size: 10.75"

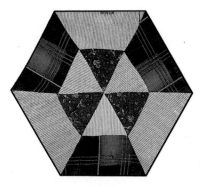

Spider Web (Old)

Accession: 38.776
Original Size: 15.25"

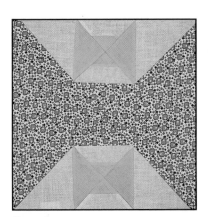

Spools

Accession: 38.23
Original Size: 10"

Springtime Blossom

Accession: 38.115
Original Size: 12"

Springtime Blossom
Lazy Daisy, Petal Quilt,
Wheel-of-Fortune

Accession: 38.391
Original Size: 9.25"

Square and Circle

Accession: 38.553
Original Size   15.5"

Square and Star

Accession: 38.124
Original size: 12"

Squares and Compass

Accession: 38.136
Original Size: 12.5"

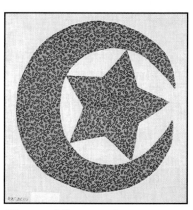

St. Louis Star

Accession: 38.311
Original size: 14"

Star and Crescent

Accession: 38.759
Original Size: 11"

Star and Cross

Accession: 38.117
Original Size: 12.5"

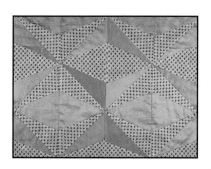

Star Fish

Accession: 38.296
Original Size: 15" x 20"

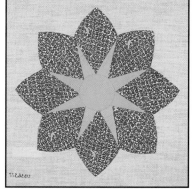

Star Flower
Golden Glow

Accession: 38.577
Original Size: 9.75

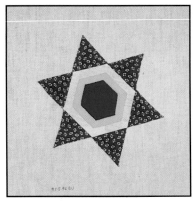

Star of Bethlehem

Accession: 38.329
Original Size: 9.75"

Star of Chamblie

Accession: 38.628
Original Size: 13.25"

Star of Hope

Accession: 38.803
Original Size 10"

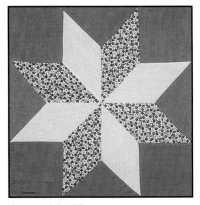

Star of LeMoyne
Lemon Star

Accession: 38.323
Original Size: 14.75"

Star of North Carolina

Accession: 38.550
Original Size: 16"

Star of the East

Accession: 38.92
Original Size: 12.5" x 10.7"

Star of the West

Accession: 38.411
Original Size: 15"

Star of the West
Compass, 4 Winds (the)

Accession: 38.837
Original Size: 11.75"

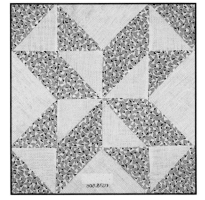

Star Puzzle

Accession: 38.806
Original Size: 10"

Starlight

Accession:	38.827
Original Size:	17"

Starry Lane

Accession:	38.128
Original Size:	12"

Stars and Planets

Accession:	38.828
Original Size:	12.5"

Stars and Squares
Rising Star

Accession:	38.345
Original Size:	15.5"

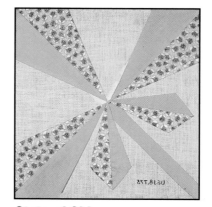

State of Ohio

Accession:	38.775
Original Size:	8.75"

Steeplechase
Bows and Arrows

Accession:	38.696
Original Size:	10"

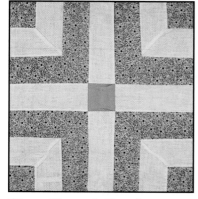

Stone Mason's Puzzle

Accession:	38.14
Original Size:	14.125"

Storm at Sea

Accession:	38.378
Original Size:	11.25"

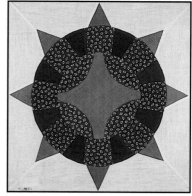

Strawberry
Kentucky Beauty

Accession:	38.17
Original Size:	11.5

String of Beads

Accession: 38.502
Original Size: 17"

String Quilt

Accession: 38.317
Original Size: 8.5"

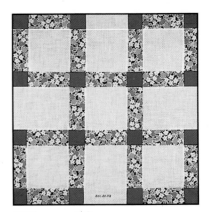

Strips and Squares

Accession: 38.168
Original Size: 16"

Sugar Bowl
Fly, Kathy's Ramble, Crow's Foot, Fan Mill

Accession: 38.460
Original Size: 8.25"

Sugar Loaf

Accession: 38.97
Original Size: 8"

Sunbeam

Accession: 38.404
Original Size: 12.25"

Sunbonnet Sue

Accession: 38.538
Original Size: 13.5"

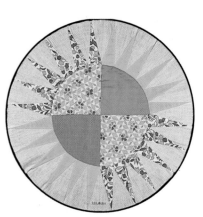

Sunburst

Accession: 38.498
Original Size: 18"

Sunburst

Accession: 38.252
Original Size: 16.5"

Sunflower

Accession: 38.499
Original Size: 18"

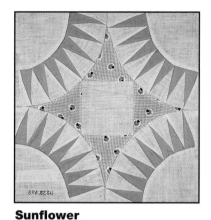

Sunflower
Indian Summer, Broken Circle

Accession: 38.698
Original Size: 9"

Sunrise

Accession: 38.587
Original Size: 10"

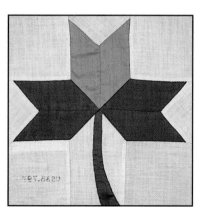

Swallow

Accession: 38.653
Original Size: 10.25"

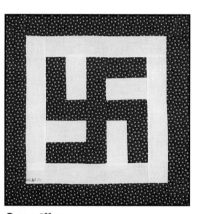

Swastika

Accession: 38.387
Original Size: 13.5"

Swastika

Accession: 38.305
Original Size: 11.5"

Sweet Gum Leaf

Accession: 38.797
Original Size: 6.5"

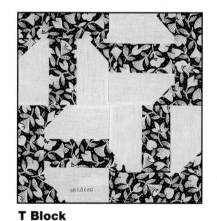

T Block

Accession: 38.380
Original Size: 10.25"

T Quartette

Accession: 38.202
Original Size: 9.25"

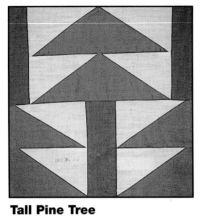

Tall Pine Tree

Accession: 38.341
Original Size: 7.5" x 8"

Tangled Garter

Accession: 38.177
Original Size: 14"

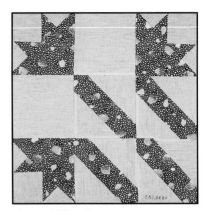

Tassel Plant

Accession: 38.383
Original Size: 11.5"

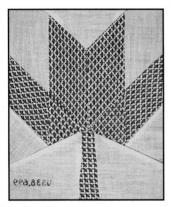

Tea Leaf

Accession: 38.699
Original Size: 5" x 6"

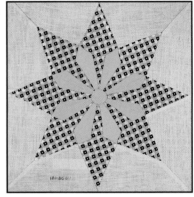

Tea Leaf

Accession: 38.578
Original Size: 9.5"

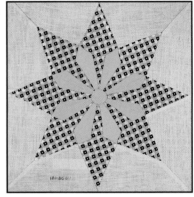

Tennessee Star

Accession: 38.481
Original Size: 9.5"

Texas Flower
Texas Treasure

Accession: 38.372
Original Size: 7.5"

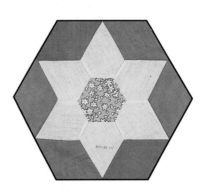

Texas Star

Accession: 38.434
Original Size: 9" x 10.25"

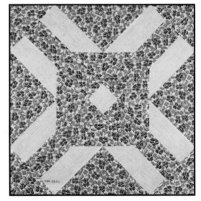

Texas Tears

Accession: 38.166
Original Size: 15.25"

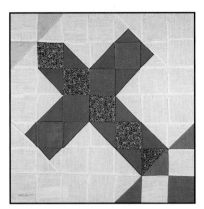

The Alta Plane

Accession: 38.634
Original Size: 14"

Thelma's Choice

Accession: 38.276
Original Size: 18"

Thunder Clouds

Accession: 38.769
Original Size: 8"

Tiger Lily

Accession: 38.726
Original Size: 12.5"

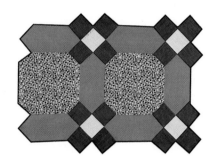

Tile Patchwork

Accession: 38.379
Original Size: 12.75" x 16"

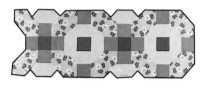

Tile Patchwork

Accession: 38.297
Original Size: 10" x 28"

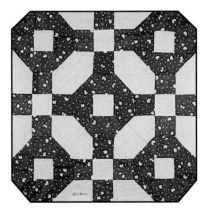

Tile Puzzle

Accession: 38.282
Original Size: 15.5"

Tiny Basket

Accession: 38.199
Original Size: 5.75"

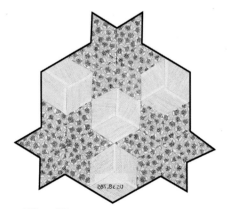

Tiny Star

Accession: 38.785
Original Size: 9" x 9.5"

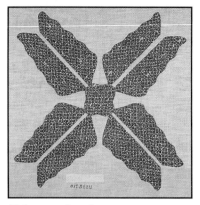

Tobacco Leaf

Accession: 38.716
Original Size: 13

Tonganoxie 9 Patch

Accession: 38.431
Original Size: 12.5"

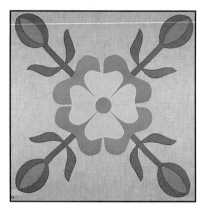

Topeka Rose

Accession: 38.821
Original Size: 18.5"

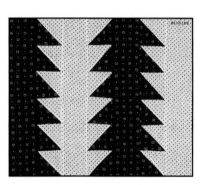

Tree Everlasting

Accession: 38.705
Original Size: 11.25" x 13"

Tree of Paradise

Accession: 38.262
Original Size: 15.5"

Tree of Paradise

Accession: 38.20
Original Size: 10.75"

Tree of Temptation

Accession: 38.250
Original Size: 12"

Triangle Puzzle

Accession: 38.91
Original Size: 9.25"

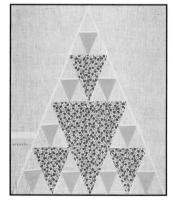

Triangular Triangles

Accession: 38.374
Original Size: 14" x 16.25"

Triple Irish Chain

Accession:	38.777
Original Size:	19"

Triple Sunflower

Accession:	38.384
Original Size:	13.5"

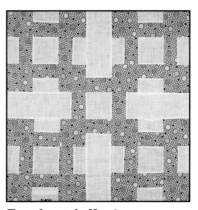

True Lover's Knot

Accession:	38.15
Original Size:	14.25"

Tulip

Accession:	38.595
Original Size:	12.25"

Tulip Appliqué

Accession:	38.581
Original Size:	8.75"

Tulip Appliqué

Accession:	38.548
Original Size:	16.25"

Tulip Garden

Accession:	38.546
Original Size:	14.5" x 15"

Tulip Lady Finger

Accession:	38.476
Original Size:	14"

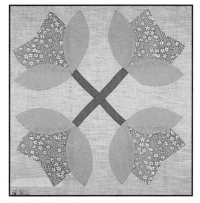

Tulip Tree Leaves

Accession:	38.762
Original Size:	14"

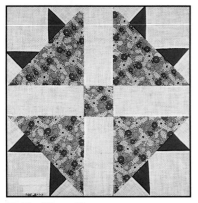

Tulip Wreath

Accession: 38.361
Original Size: 14"

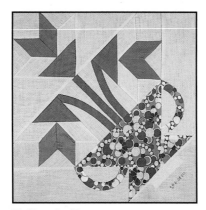

Tulips in Vase
Royal Japanese Vase

Accession: 38.492
Original Size: 12.75"

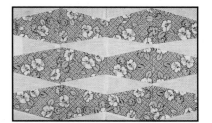

Tumbler

Accession: 38.706
Original Size: 9.5" x 15.5"

Turnabout T

Accession: 38.48
Original Size: 14"

Twin Sisters

Accession: 38.458
Original Size: 8"

Twinkling Star
Star & Crescent

Accession: 38.591
Original Size: 12.5" x 14"

Union Star

Accession: 38.88
Original Size: 10.5"

Urn (The)

Accession: 38.543
Original Size: 13.5"

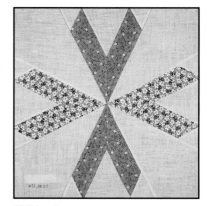

V Block

Accession: 38.126
Original Size: 11.75"

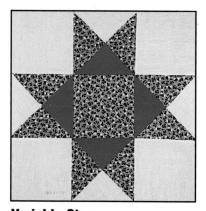

Variable Star

Accession: 38.661
Original Size: 12"

Vase of Autumn Leaves

Accession: 38.599
Original Size: 11"

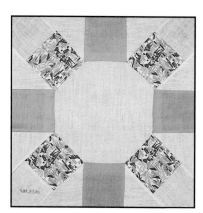

Venetian Design

Accession: 38.367
Original Size: 10"

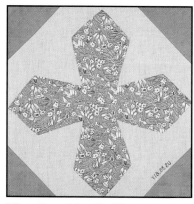

Vice President's Star

Accession: 38.817
Original Size: 11.25"

Village Church

Accession: 38.520
Original Size: 13.25" x 20"

Vine of Friendship

Accession: 38.337
Original Size: 14.75"

Virginia Rose

Accession: 38.733
Original Size: 18"

Virginia Star
Star Upon Stars

Accession: 38.313
Original Size: 16"

Walk Around

Accession: 38.464
Original Size: 11" x 13"

Wandering Foot
Turkey Tracks

Accession: 38.708
Original Size: 16.5"

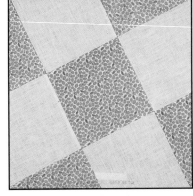

Washington's Puzzle

Accession: 38.422
Original Size: 10.5"

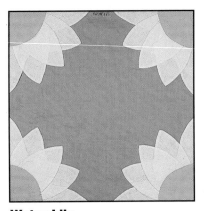

Water Lily

Accession: 38.532
Original Size: 12.25"

Way of the World

Accession: 38.780
Original Size: 10"

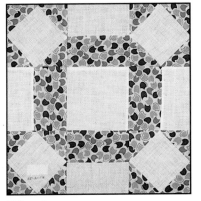

Wheel
Single Wedding Ring

Accession: 38.452
Original Size: 10.5"

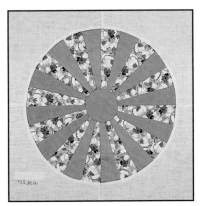

Wheel of Chance
True Lover's Buggy Wheel

Accession: 38.237
Original Size: 12"

Wheel of Fortune

Accession: 38.369
Original Size: 13.5"

Wheel of Mystery
Winding Ways

Accession: 38.802
Original Size: 15.25"

Whig Rose

Accession: 38.709
Original Size: 19.25"

Whig Rose

Accession: 38.731
Original Size: 16"

Whig's Defeat

Accession: 38.524
Original Size: 21"

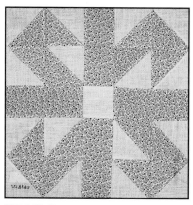

Whirligig

Accession: 38.157
Original Size: 11.25"

Whirligig

Accession: 38.64
Original Size: 12"

Whirling Legs

Accession: 38.767
Original Size: 8.25"

White Cloud

Accession: 38.309
Original Size: 8.25"

White House Steps

Accession: 38.271
Original Size: 12"

White Rose

Accession: 38.69
Original Size: 15"

Widow's Mite

Accession: 38.326
Original Size: 15"

Widower's Choice

Accession: 38.125
Original Size: 12"

Wild Goose

Accession: 38.146
Original Size: 11"

Wild Rose

Accession: 38.838
Original Size: 16.75" x 22"

Wild Rose

Accession: 38.545
Original Size: 16" x 16.75"

Wild Rose

Accession: 38.823
Original Size: 21"

Wind Blown Rose

Accession: 38.512
Original Size: 17"

Wind Blown Tulips

Accession: 38.516
Original Size: 17"

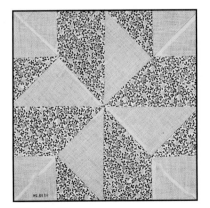

Windmill

Accession: 38.24
Original Size: 9.75"

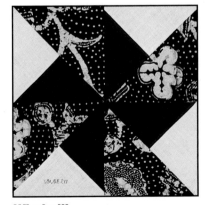

Windmill

Accession: 38.187
Original Size: 9"

Windmill Star
Amethyst

Accession: 38.565
Original Size: 11.75" x 12"

Wonder of the World

Accession: 38.335
Original Size: 11.5"

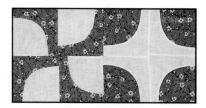

Wonder of the World

Accession: 38.466
Original Size: 8" x 16"

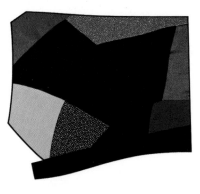

Wool Crazy Quilt

Accession: 38.465
Original Size: 17" x 14"

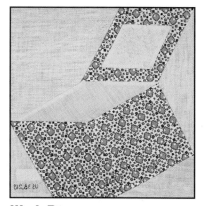

Work Box

Accession: 38.218
Original Size: 7.75"

World Without End
Priscilla

Accession: 38.703
Original Size: 16"

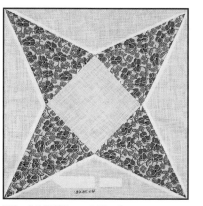

World Without End
Priscilla

Accession: 38.681
Original Size: 10.75"

World's Fair

Accession: 38.388
Original Size: 11.75"

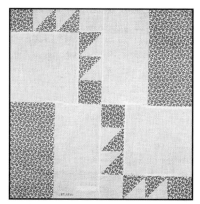

World's Fair Puzzle

Accession: 38.76
Original Size: 15"

Wreath of Carnations

Accession: 38.505
Original Size: 19.25"

Wreath of Pansies

Accession: 38.562
Original Size: 16"

Wreath of Roses
Garden Wreath

Accession: 38.522
Original Size: 19"

Wreath of Wild Roses

Accession: 38.563
Original Size: 14.25"

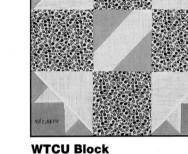

WTCU Block

Accession: 38.389
Original Size: 9.25"

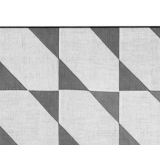

X-quisite

Accession: 38.134
Original Size: 13"

Yankee Puzzle

Accession: 38.347
Original Size: 12"

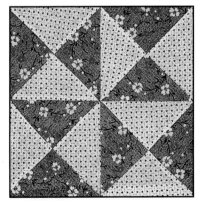

Yankee Puzzle

Accession: 38.665
Original Size: 7.75"

Zig Zag
Streak of Lightning

Accession: 38.676
Original Size: 9.5" x 12.5"

Patterned Blocks

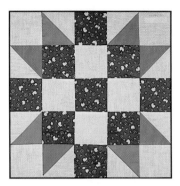

4 X Star

Accession: 38.474
Original Size: 12.75"
Pattern Size: 12.5"
Templates:
A2.5   B2.5

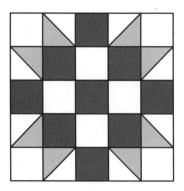

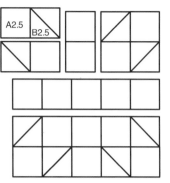

54-40 or Fight

Accession: 38.645
Original Size: 12.25"
Pattern Size: 12"
Templates:
A2   T1   T2
T2r

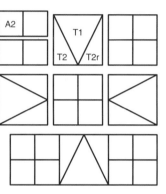

Ah' Teen

Accession: 38.772
Original Size: 8"
Pattern Size: 8"
Templates:
A1   B1   B2
C2   T3   T4
T5   T5r   T6
T6r

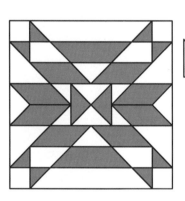

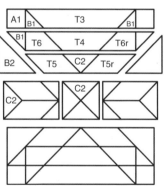

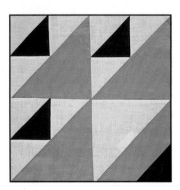

Aircraft

Accession: 38.478
Original Size: 10.75"
Pattern Size: 10"
Templates:
B2.5   B5   T7

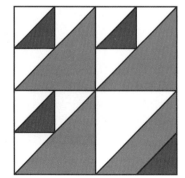

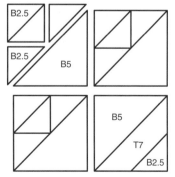

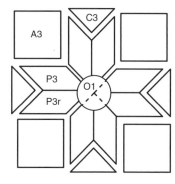
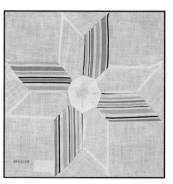

Album

Accession: 38.454
Original Size: 8"
Pattern Size: 9"
Templates:

A3	C3	O1
P3	P3r	

Appliqué O1 to the center of the block.

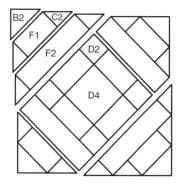

Album

Accession: 38.419
Original Size: 10.75"
Pattern Size: 10"
Templates:

B2	C2	D2
D4	F1	F2

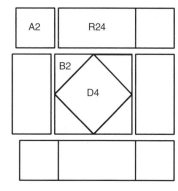
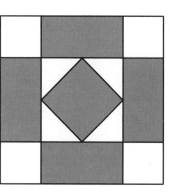

Album

Accession: 38.448
Original Size: 8.25"
Pattern Size: 8"
Templates:

A2	B2	D4
R24		

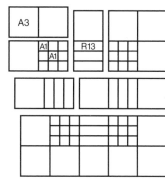
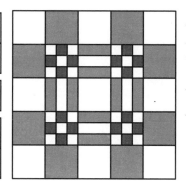
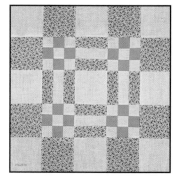

Album Patch

Accession: 38.275
Original Size: 15"
Pattern Size: 15"
Templates:

A1	A3	R13

All Kinds

Accession:	38.49	
Original Size:	12"	
Pattern Size:	12"	
Templates:		
B2	C2	C4
F3	T8	

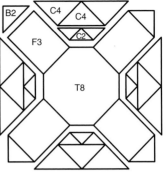

Amethyst

Accession:	38.398	
Original Size:	13.75"	
Pattern Size:	12"	
Templates:		
D3	T9	T10
T11		

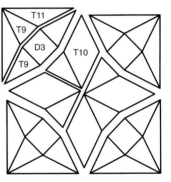

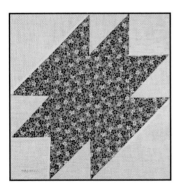

Anvil

Accession:	38.659	
Original Size:	10.25"	
Pattern Size:	10"	
Templates:		
A2.5	A5	B2.5
B5		

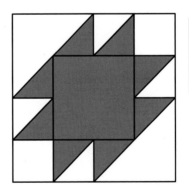

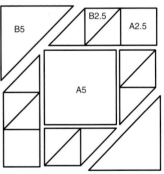

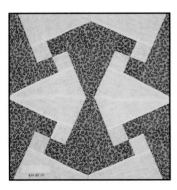

Arabic Lattice

Accession:	38.101	
Original Size:	9.5"	
Pattern Size:	10"	
Templates:		
T12	T13	T13r

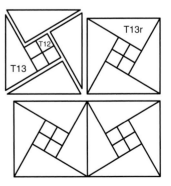

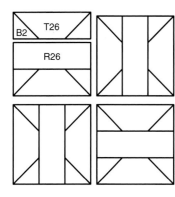
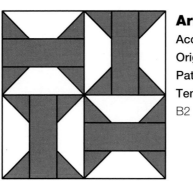

Arkansas Traveler

Accession: 38.51

Original Size: 12"

Pattern Size: 12"

Templates:

B2   R26   T26

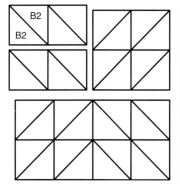
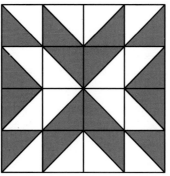
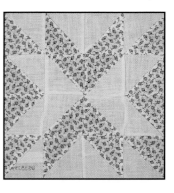

Arrow Point

Accession: 38.799

Original Size: 8.25"

Pattern Size: 8"

Templates:

B2

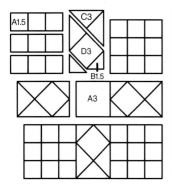

Arrowhead

Accession: 38.54

Original Size: 13"

Pattern Size: 12"

Templates:

A1.5   A3   B1.5

C3   D3

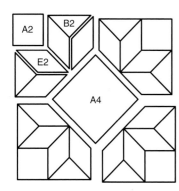

Arrowhead Star

Accession: 38.790

Original Size: 9.25"

Pattern Size: 9.65"

Templates:

A2   A4   B2

E2

Art Square

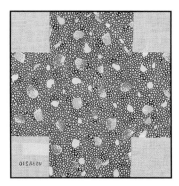

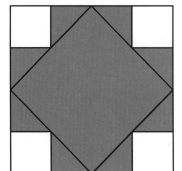

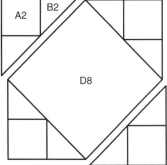

Accession: 38.210
Original Size: 8.5"
Pattern Size: 8"
Templates:
A2   B2   D8

Aunt Sukey's Choice

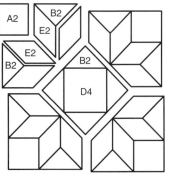

Accession: 38.366
Original Size: 10"
Pattern Size: 9.65"
Templates:
A2   B2   D4
E2

Autograph Patch

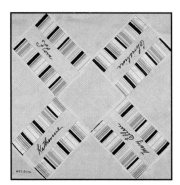

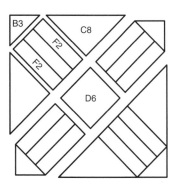

Accession: 38.394
Original Size: 13.5"
Pattern Size: 14"
Templates:
B3   C8   D6
F2

Autumn Leaf
Maple Leaf

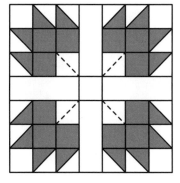

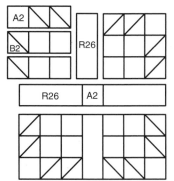

Accession: 38.674
Original Size: 12.5"
Pattern Size: 14"
Templates:
A2   B2   R26

Applique ½" stems as shown by dotted lines.

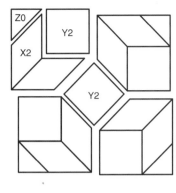

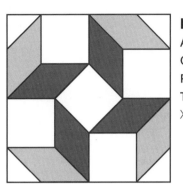

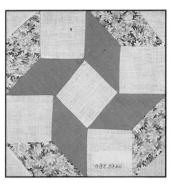

Bachelor's Puzzle

Accession: 38.386
Original Size: 8"
Pattern Size: 8"
Templates:

X2   Y2   Z0

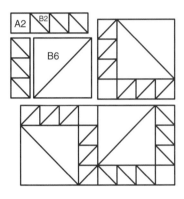

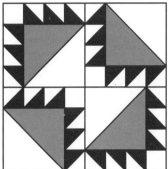

Barrister's Block

Lawyer's Puzzle

Accession: 38.13
Original Size: 14.25"
Pattern Size: 16"
Templates:

A2   B2   B6

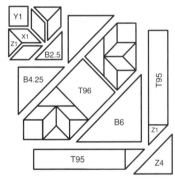

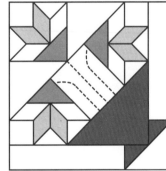

Basket of Lilies

Basket of Tulips

Accession: 38.370
Original Size: 12.5"
Pattern Size: 12"
Templates:

B2.5   B4.25   B6
T95   T96   X1
Y1   Z1   Z4

Appliqué ½" bias stems as shown by dotted lines.

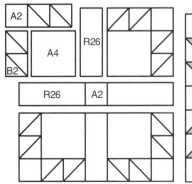

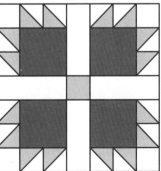

Bear's Paw

Accession: 38.641
Original Size: 12.25"
Pattern Size: 14"
Templates:

A2   A4   B2
R26

Beautiful Star

Accession: 38.788
Original Size: 10"
Pattern Size: 10"
Templates:

T19   T101   T102

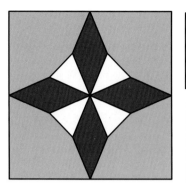

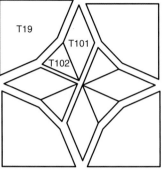

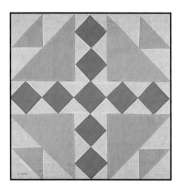

Beggar's Block

Accession: 38.135
Original Size: 11.25"
Pattern Size: 9"
Templates:

A3   B1   R13
T20

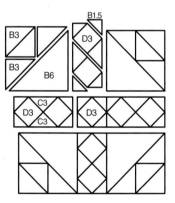

Bird's Nest

Accession: 38.70
Original Size: 14.5"
Pattern Size: 15"
Templates:

B1.5   B3   B6
C3   D3

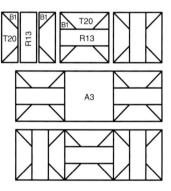

Birds in the Air

Accession: 38.657
Original Size: 9.25"
Pattern Size: 9"
Templates:

B1.5   B4.5

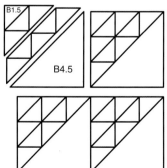

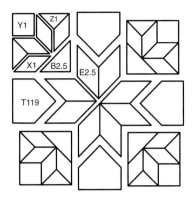

Blazing Star

Accession: 38.68
Original Size: 12.5"
Pattern Size: 12"
Templates:

B2.5	E2.5	T119
X1	Y1	Z1

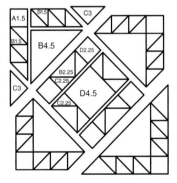

Blazing Star

Accession: 38.418
Original Size: 14"
Pattern Size: 12"
Templates:

T107	T117	X1
Z1		

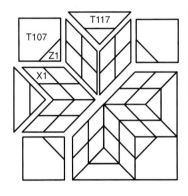

Blind Man's Fancy

Accession: 38.141
Original Size: 12"
Pattern Size: 12"
Templates:

A1.5	B1.5	B2.25
B4.5	C2.25	C3
D2.25	D4.5	

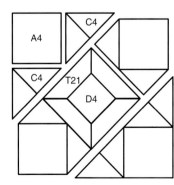
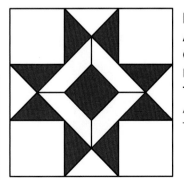

Braced Star

Accession: 38.428
Original Size: 12.25"
Pattern Size: 12"
Templates:

A4	C4	D4
T21		

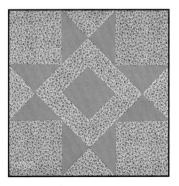

Brown Goose
Double Z
Accession: 38.656
Original Size: 11.25"
Pattern Size: 12"
Templates:
B3   C6

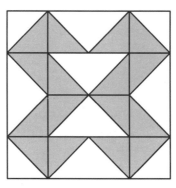

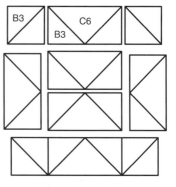

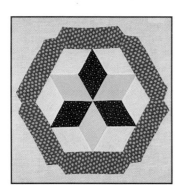

Brunswick Star
Rolling Star, Chained Star
Accession: 38.331
Original Size: 15.25"
Pattern Size: 15"
Appliqué block to background square. 15"
Templates:
G2   T22

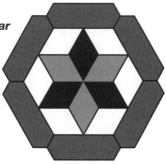

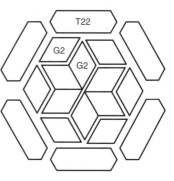

Burgoyne Surrounded
Accession: 38.442
Original Size: 15.5"
Pattern Size: 15"
Templates:
A1   A2   R12
R13   R16   R35
Sashing strips, as shown, are needed to complete the pattern.

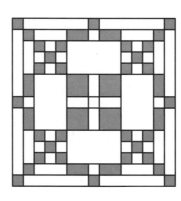

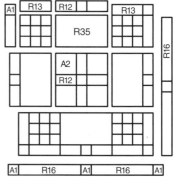

Cactus Basket
Accession: 38.778
Original Size: 8"
Pattern Size: 8.82"
Templates:
A2   B2   B4
E2   T115   T116

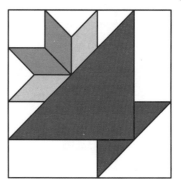

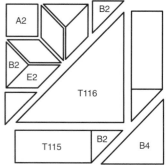

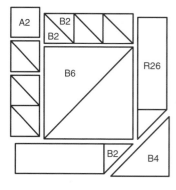

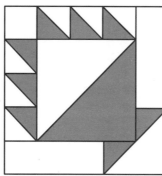

Cake Stand

Accession: 38.37
Original Size: 10.25"
Pattern Size: 10"
Templates:

A2	B2	B4
B6	R26	

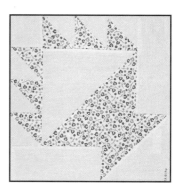

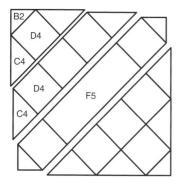

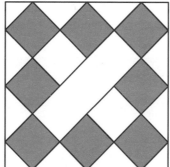

Carrie Hall Album

Accession: 38.225
Original Size: 10.5"
Pattern Size: 12"
Templates:

B2	C4	D4
F5		

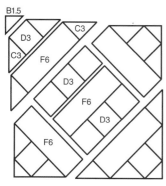

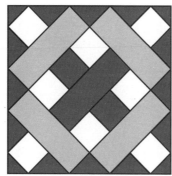

Casement Window

Accession: 38.447
Original Size: 12.25"
Pattern Size: 12"
Templates:

B1.5	C3	D3
F6		

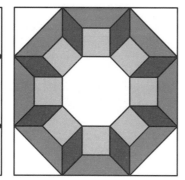

Castle Wall

Accession: 38.441
Original Size: 12.75"
Pattern Size: 11.66"
Templates:

A2	E2	T121
T122	T123	

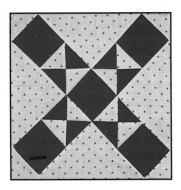

Cats and Mice

Accession: 38.254

Original Size: 10.25"

Pattern Size: 12"

Templates:

B2   C8   D4

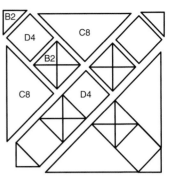

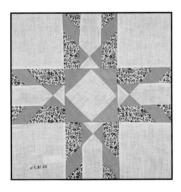

Chicago Star

Accession: 38.216

Original Size: 11.25"

Pattern Size: 9"

Templates:

A3   B1   B1.5

C1   D3   R12

T23   T23r   T24

T24r

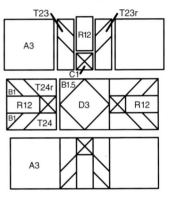

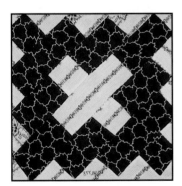

Chimney Sweep

Accession: 38.773

Original Size: 9"

Pattern Size: 8"

Templates:

B1   C2   D2

F1   F7

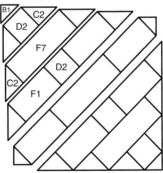

Chinese Coin

Accession: 38.626

Original Size: 12.5"

Pattern Size: 12"

Templates:

A1.5   A3   B3

R159

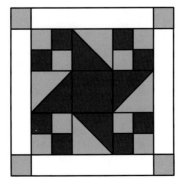

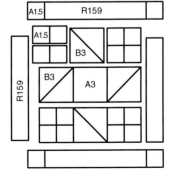

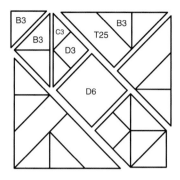

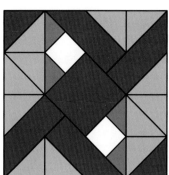

Chinese Puzzle

Accession: 38.624
Original Size: 12.5"
Pattern Size: 12"
Templates:

B3	C3	D3
D6	T25	

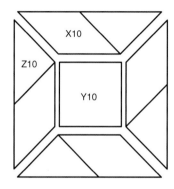

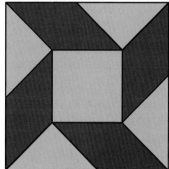

Churn Dash

Accession: 38.764
Original Size: 9.75"
Pattern Size: 10"
Templates:

X10	Y10	Z10

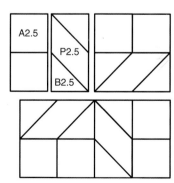

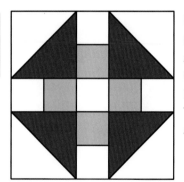

Churn Dash
Churn Dasher

Accession: 38.324
Original Size: 7.5"
Pattern Size: 7.5"
Templates:

A1.5	B3

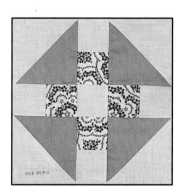

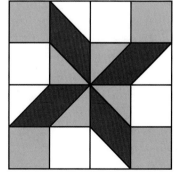

Clay's Choice

Accession: 38.444
Original Size: 10"
Pattern Size: 10"
Templates:

A2.5	B2.5	P2.5

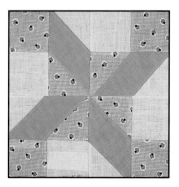

Clown's Choice

Accession: 38.132

Original Size: 13"

Pattern Size: 15"

Templates:

A3   C3

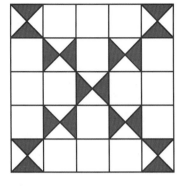

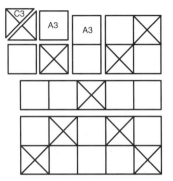

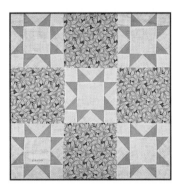

Cluster of Stars

Accession: 38.338

Original Size: 17.5"

Pattern Size: 18"

Templates:

A1.5   A3   A6

B1.5   C3

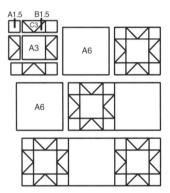

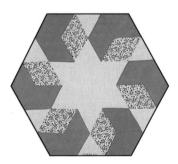

Columbia Star

Accession: 38.604

Original Size: 13.75"

Pattern Size: 12" x 10.4"

Templates:

G2   I2

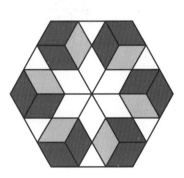

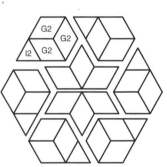

Corn and Beans

Shoo Fly, Handy Andy,
Hen and Chickens,
Duck and Ducklings

Accession: 38.244

Original Size: 12"

Pattern Size: 12"

Templates:

B2   B4   C4

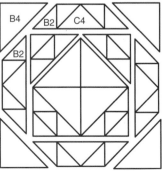

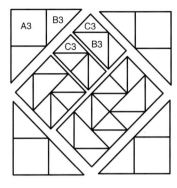

Crazy Ann

Accession: 38.53
Original Size: 12"
Pattern Size: 12"
Templates:
A3　　　B3　　　C3

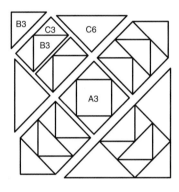

Crimson Rambler
Spring Beauty

Accession: 38.63
Original Size: 12"
Pattern Size: 12"
Templates:
A3　　　B3　　　C3
C6

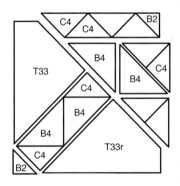
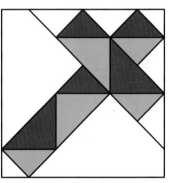

Cross

Accession: 38.396
Original Size: 12.5"
Pattern Size: 12"
Templates:
B2　　　B4　　　C4
T33　　　T33r

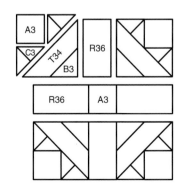

Cross and Crown

Accession: 38.72
Original Size: 14.5"
Pattern Size: 15"
Templates:
A3　　　B3　　　C3
R36　　　T34

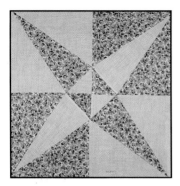

Crossed Canoes

Accession: 38.420

Original Size: 14"

Pattern Size: 12"

Templates:

B2   T35   T35r

T36

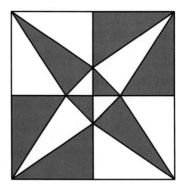

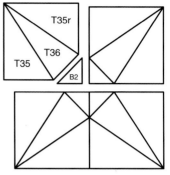

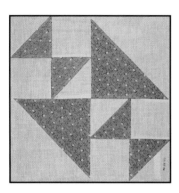

Crosses and Losses

Fox and Geese

Accession: 38.45

Original Size: 12"

Pattern Size: 12"

Templates:

A3   B3   B6

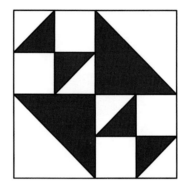

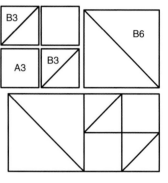

Crossroads to Texas

Accession: 38.137

Original Size: 17"

Pattern Size: 18"

Templates:

B4.5   C3   C9

D3   F6

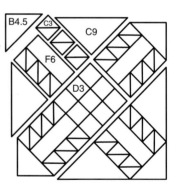

Crown of Thorns

Single Wedding Ring

Accession: 38.120

Original Size: 10"

Pattern Size: 10"

Templates:

A2   B2

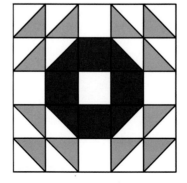

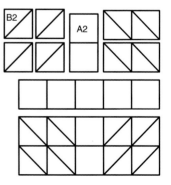

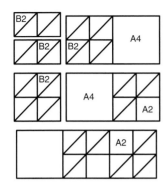

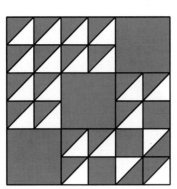

Cut Glass Dish

Accession: 38.439
Original Size: 12.25"
Pattern Size: 12"
Templates:

A2   A4   B2

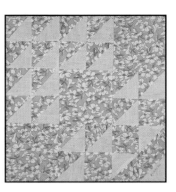

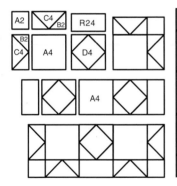

Delectable Mountains

Accession: 38.685
Original Size: 14.25"
Pattern Size: 14"
Templates:

B7   C1   C6
D1   X1   Y1
Z1

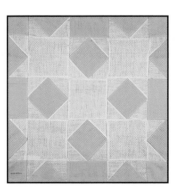

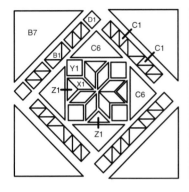

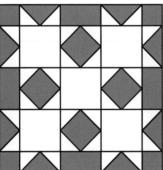

Devil's Claws

Accession: 38.406
Original Size: 16.5"
Pattern Size: 16"
Templates:

A2   A4   B2
C4   D4   R24

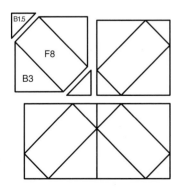

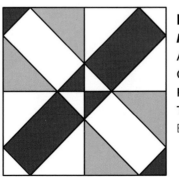

Devil's Puzzle
Fly Foot

Accession: 38.144
Original Size: 7.5"
Pattern Size: 9"
Templates:

B1.5   B3   F8

Diamond Star

Accession: 38.805
Original Size: 11.25"
Pattern Size: 12"
Templates:
A3   C3   P3
P3r

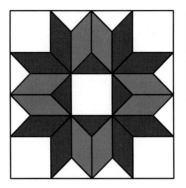

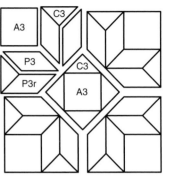

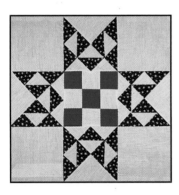

Dolly Madison's Star

Accession: 38.98
Original Size: 18"
Pattern Size: 18"
Templates:
A2   A6   C3
C6

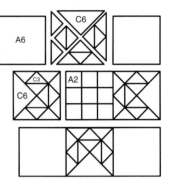

Domino

Accession: 38.116
Original Size: 12.25"
Pattern Size: 12"
Templates:
A2   A4   R24

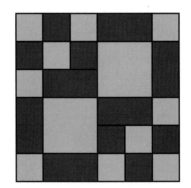

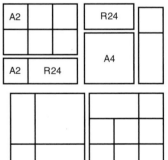

Domino and Square

Accession: 38.164
Original Size: 14.25"
Pattern Size: 15"
Templates:
B3   C3   D3
D6   F8

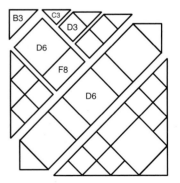

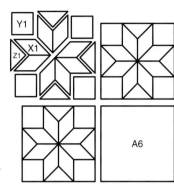

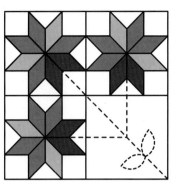

Double Peony

Accession: 38.575

Original Size: 12.5"

Pattern Size: 12"

Templates:

A6   X1   Y1

Z1

Appliqué ½" bias stems and two leaves as shown by dashed lines (pg.136).

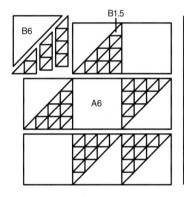

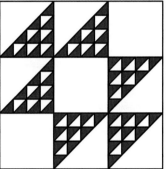

Double Pyramid

Accession: 38.671

Original Size: 17.25"

Pattern Size: 18"

Templates:

A6   B1.5   B6

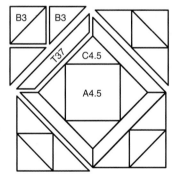

Double Square

Accession: 38.195

Original Size: 10.5"

Pattern Size: 12"

Templates:

A4.5   B3   C4.5

T37

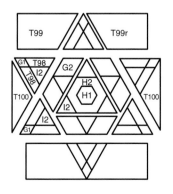

Double Star

Accession: 38.306

Original Size: 12.25" x 14"

Pattern Size: 12.11" x 14"

Templates:

H1   H2   G1

G2   I2   T98

T99   T99r   T100

Appliqué small hexagon (H1) on H2.

Double Star
Star Within a Star, Carpenter's Star
Accession: 38.152
Original Size: 12.25"
Pattern Size: 12"
Templates:
X1 Y1 Z1

Double X
Accession: 38.615
Original Size: 6.5"
Pattern Size: 6"
Templates:
A1.5 A3 B1.5

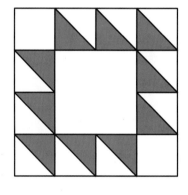

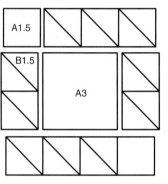

Double X
Accession: 38.489B
Original Size: 8.25"
Pattern Size: 8"
Templates:
A2 B2 B4

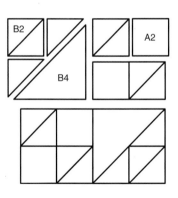

Double X
Accession: 38.489C
Original Size: 9"
Pattern Size: 9"
Templates:
A1.5 A3 B1.5
B3 C3

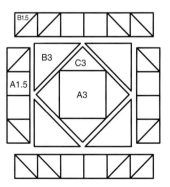

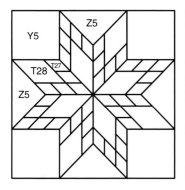

Dove in the Window

Accession: 38.82

Original Size: 14"

Pattern Size: 14"

Templates:

T27	T28	Y5
Z5		

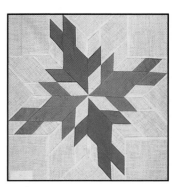

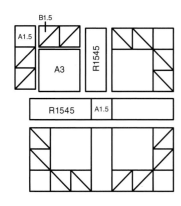

Dove in the Window

Accession: 38.774

Original Size: 10.75"

Pattern Size: 10.5"

Templates:

A1.5	A3	B1.5
R1545		

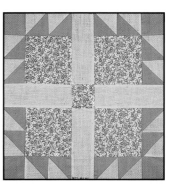

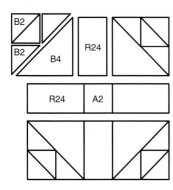

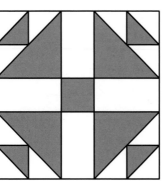

Duck and Ducklings
Corn and Beans

Accession: 38.67

Original Size: 12"

Pattern Size: 10"

Templates:

A2	B2	B4
R24		

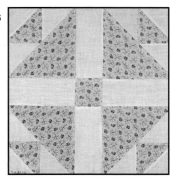

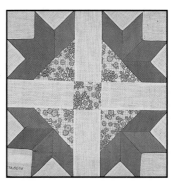

Duck Paddle
Fannie's Fan

Accession: 38.377

Original Size: 11.5"

Pattern Size: 10"

Templates:

A1.5	B2.5	T39
X1	Y1	Z1

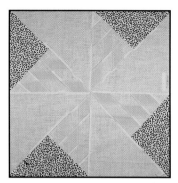

Dutch Windmill

Accession: 38.407

Original Size: 16"

Pattern Size: 16"

Templates:

B8	C2	C8
P2		

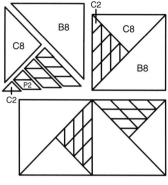

Dutchman's Puzzle

Accession: 38.437

Original Size: 9"

Pattern Size: 8"

Templates:

B2	C4

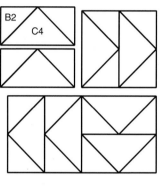

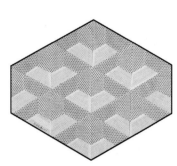

Ecclesiastical

Accession: 38.268

Original Size: 10.75" x 12.75"

Pattern Size: 9" x 10.4"

Template: K1

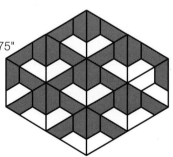

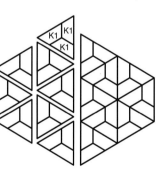

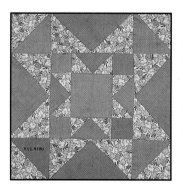

Eight Hands Around

Accession: 38.229

Original Size: 12"

Pattern Size: 12"

Templates:

A1.5	A3	B1.5
B3	C3	C6

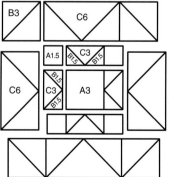

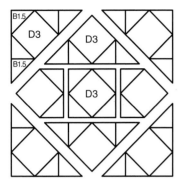

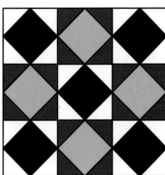

Eight Point All Over

Accession:	38.208
Original Size:	9"
Pattern Size:	9"

Templates:

B1.5　　D3

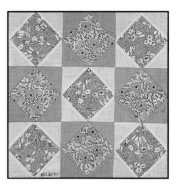

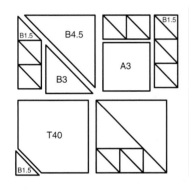

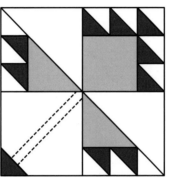

English Ivy

Accession:	38.105
Original Size:	9"
Pattern Size:	9"

Templates:

A3　　　B1.5　　B3

B4.5　　T40

Appliqué ½" bias stem as shown by dashed line.

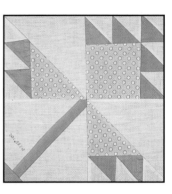

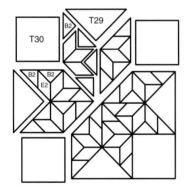

Falling Star
Flying Swallows

Accession:	38.417
Original Size:	14.5"
Pattern Size:	16.5"

Templates:

B2　　　E2　　　T29

T30

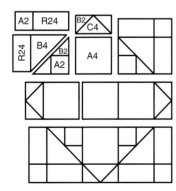

Fanny's Favorite

Accession:	38.170
Original Size:	16"
Pattern Size:	16"

Templates:

A2　　　A4　　　B2

B4　　　C4　　　R24

Five Diamonds

Accession: 38.106
Original Size: 9.75"
Pattern Size: 9"
Templates:
B1.5   B3   C3
D3

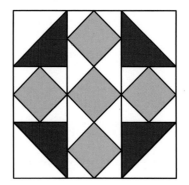

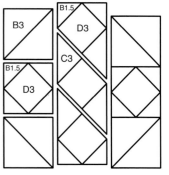

Flock of Geese

Accession: 38.689
Original Size: 12"
Pattern Size: 12"
Templates:
B3   B6

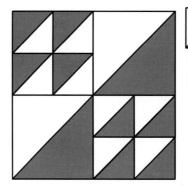

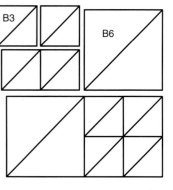

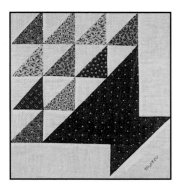

Flower Pot

Accession: 38.197
Original Size: 10"
Pattern Size: 10"
Templates:
B2   B4   B6
R26

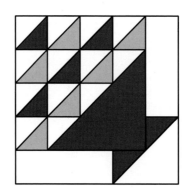

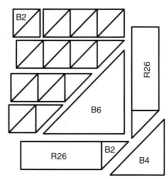

Flower Pot

Accession: 38.354
Original Size: 10.5"
Pattern Size: 10.5"
Templates:
B2   B4   B5
R265   X1   Y4
Z4

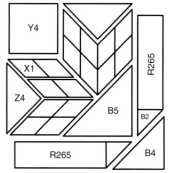

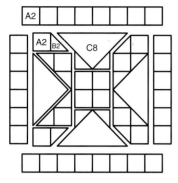

Flying Clouds

Accession: 38.678
Original Size: 14.25"
Pattern Size: 16"
Templates:
A2   B2   C8

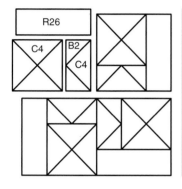

Flying Dutchman

Accession: 38.339
Original Size: 17"
Pattern Size: 12"
Templates:
B2   C4   R26

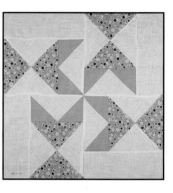

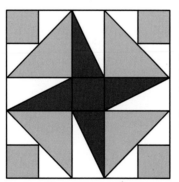

Follow the Leader

Accession: 38.669
Original Size: 9"
Pattern Size: 10"
Templates:
A2   B2   B4
T42

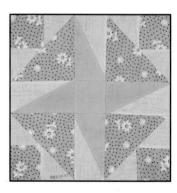

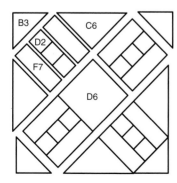

Four H Club Patch

Accession: 38.303
Original Size: 13.75"
Pattern Size: 12"
Templates:
B3   C6   D2
D6   F7

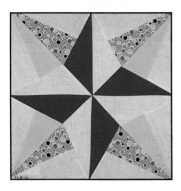

Four Pointed Star
Blazing Star
Accession: 38.29
Original Size: 11"
Pattern Size: 12"
Templates:

T43	T43r	T44
T44r	T45	T45r

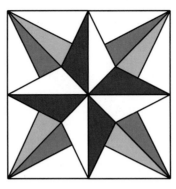

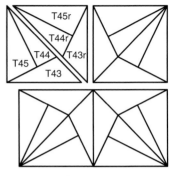

Free Trade Patch
Accession: 38.666
Original Size: 14"
Pattern Size: 16"
Templates:

A2	B2	B4
C8		

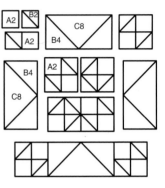

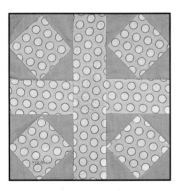

Garden of Eden
Accession: 38.479
Original Size: 9.25"
Pattern Size: 10"
Templates:

B2	D4	R24
R210		

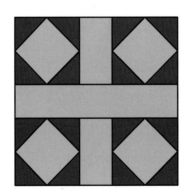

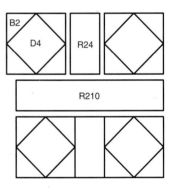

Gentleman's Fancy
Accession: 38.446
Original Size: 12.25"
Pattern Size: 12"
Templates:

A4	B4	C4

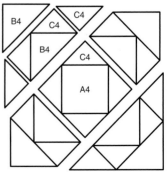

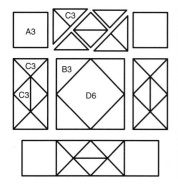

Georgetown Circle

Accession: 38.691
Original Size: 12"
Pattern Size: 12"
Templates:

A3	B3	C3
D6		

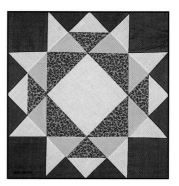

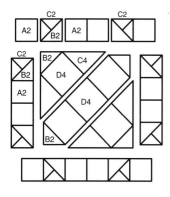

Golgotha

*3 Crosses,
Cross Upon Cross*

Accession: 38.682
Original Size: 13"
Pattern Size: 12"
Templates:

A2	B2	C2
C4	D4	

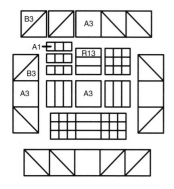

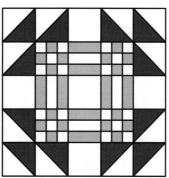

Goose in the Pond

Young Man's Fancy

Accession: 38.680
Original Size: 15.5"
Pattern Size: 15"
Templates:

A1	A3	B3
R13		

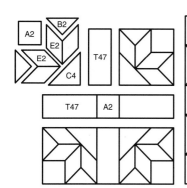

Goose Tracks

Accession: 38.477
Original Size: 13"
Pattern Size: 11.65"
Templates:

A2	B2	C4
E2	T47	

Goose Tracks

Accession: 38.359

Original Size: 10"

Pattern Size: 10"

Templates:

A2   B4   C2

R24

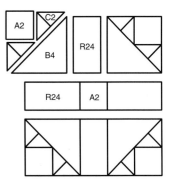

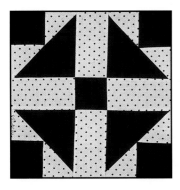

Grandmother's Choice

Accession: 38.220

Original Size: 12"

Pattern Size: 10"

Templates:

A2   B2   B4

R24

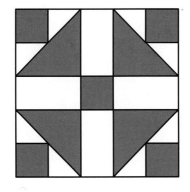

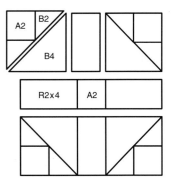

Grandmother's Favorite

Accession: 38.348

Original Size: 12"

Pattern Size: 12"

Templates:

A6   B3   C3

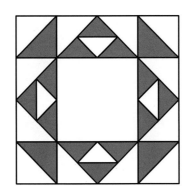

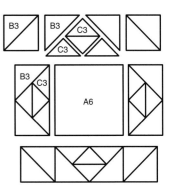

Grape Basket

Accession: 38.26

Original Size: 10"

Pattern Size: 10"

Templates:

A2   B2   B4

R26

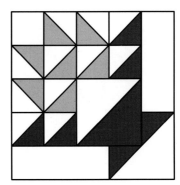

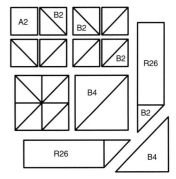

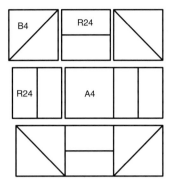

Grecian Design

Accession: 38.52

Original Size: 12.5"

Pattern Size: 12"

Templates:

A4   B4   R24

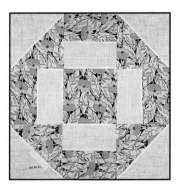

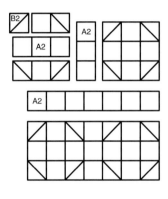

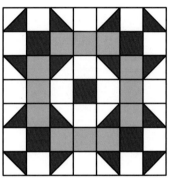

Greek Cross

Accession: 38.787

Original Size: 17.5"

Pattern Size: 14"

Templates:

A2   B2

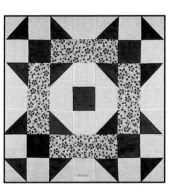

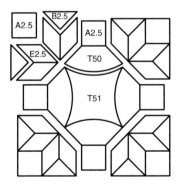

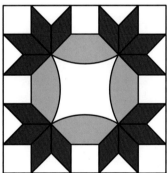

Hands All Around

Accession: 38.114

Original Size: 14.25"

Pattern Size: 12.5"

Templates:

A2.5   B2.5   E2.5

T50   T51

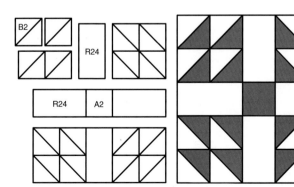

Handy Andy

Accession: 38.697

Original Size: 9"

Pattern Size: 10"

Templates:

A2   B2   R24

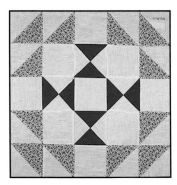

Handy Andy

Accession: 38.245
Original Size: 15"
Pattern Size: 15"
Templates:
A3   B3   C3

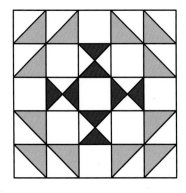

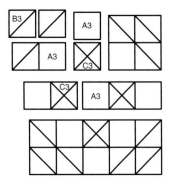

Hen and Chickens

Accession: 38.143
Original Size: 10.5"
Pattern Size: 10.5"
Templates:
A1.5   A3   B1.5
R1545

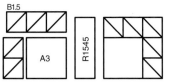

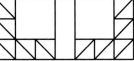

Hexagonal Star
Rising Star

Accession: 38.196
Original Size: 10.5" x 11.75"
Pattern Size: 12" x 10.4"
Template: G3

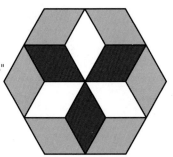

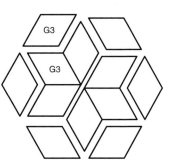

Hovering Hawks

Accession: 38.650
Original Size: 10.25"
Pattern Size: 10"
Templates:
A2.5   B2.5   B5

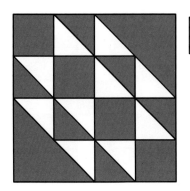

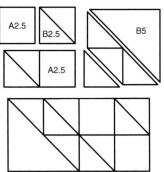

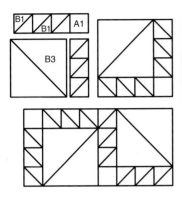

Indian Trails

Accession: 38.424

Original Size: 9.25"

Pattern Size: 8"

Templates:

A1   B1   B3

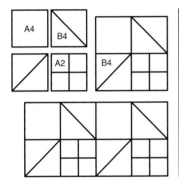

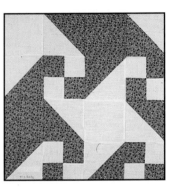

Indiana Puzzle

Accession: 38.179

Original Size: 15.5"

Pattern Size: 16"

Templates:

A2   A4   B4

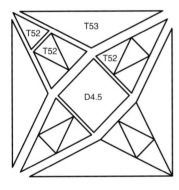

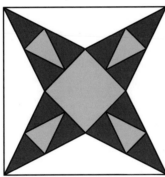

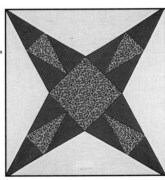

Iowa Star

Accession: 38.320

Original Size: 14.25" x 14.5"

Pattern Size: 9"

Templates:

D4.5   T52   T53

Irish Puzzle

Blue and White

Accession: 38.19

Original Size: 16"

Pattern Size: 16"

Templates:

A2   B2   B6

D4

Jack-in-the-Box
Whirligig

Accession: 38.403
Original Size: 10.5"
Pattern Size: 10"
Templates:

A2	B2	C4
P4	R24	

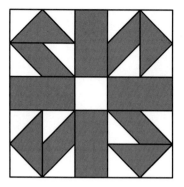

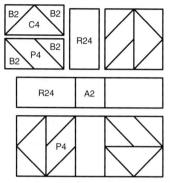

Jack in the Pulpit
Toad in the Puddle

Accession: 38.810
Original Size: 8"
Pattern Size: 12"
Templates:

A3.5	B3	C3.5
D2.5	F9	

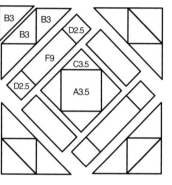

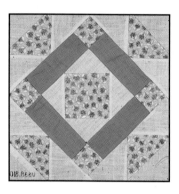

Jackson Star
4 Stars

Accession: 38.349
Original Size: 13.5"
Pattern Size: 12"
Templates:

X1	Y1	Z1

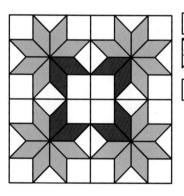

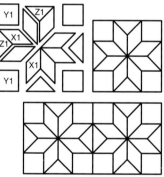

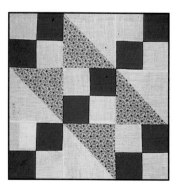

Jacob's Ladder
Railroad

Accession: 38.328
Original Size: 13.5"
Pattern Size: 12"
Templates:

A2	B4

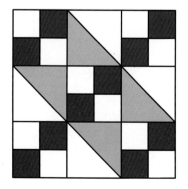

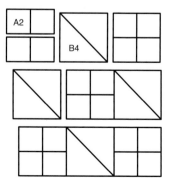

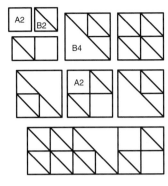

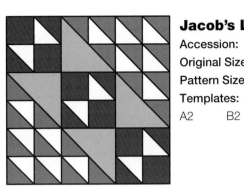

Jacob's Ladder

Accession: 38.617

Original Size: 11.5" x 12.5"

Pattern Size: 12"

Templates:

A2   B2   B4

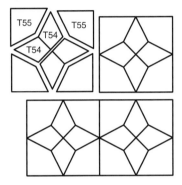

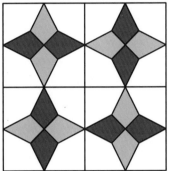

Job's Troubles

Accession: 38.421

Original Size: 10.25"

Pattern Size: 12"

Templates:

T54   T55

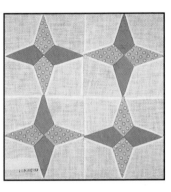

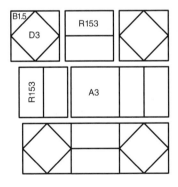

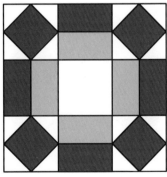

Johnnie Round the Corner

Single Wedding Ring, Wheel

Accession: 38.260

Original Size: 9.25"

Pattern Size: 9"

Templates:

A3   B1.5   D3

R153

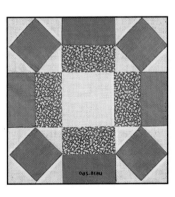

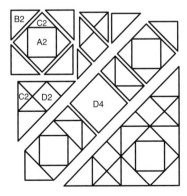

Joseph's Coat

Accession: 38.94

Original Size: 9.25"

Pattern Size: 10"

Templates:

A2   B2   C2

D2   D4

Kansas Dust Storm

Kansas City Star

Accession: 38.393
Original Size: 12.25"
Pattern Size: 12"
Templates:

A2.5	C5	E2.5
T57	T58	

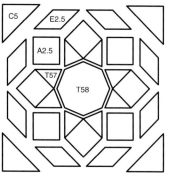

Kansas Star

Accession: 38.42
Original Size: 12"
Pattern Size: 12"
Templates:

B2	D4

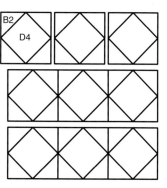

Kansas Troubles

Accession: 38.233
Original Size: 12.25"
Pattern Size: 12"
Templates:

A1.5	B1.5	B3
B6		

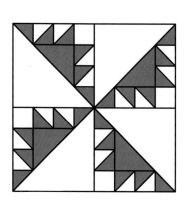

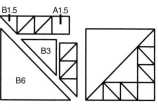

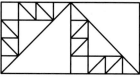

Ladies Delight

Accession: 38.73
Original Size: 15"
Pattern Size: 15"
Templates:

A1.5	A3	B1.5
B3	C3	T59
T60	T60r	

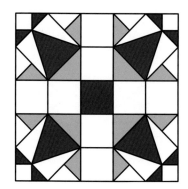

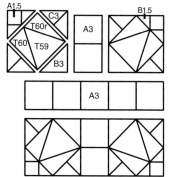

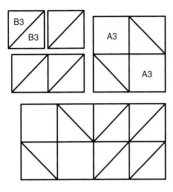 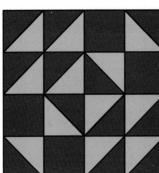 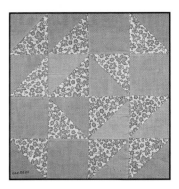

Ladies' Wreath

Accession: 38.360
Original Size: 12"
Pattern Size: 12"
Templates:
A3   B3

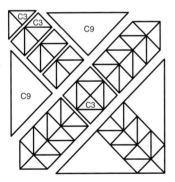 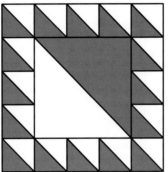 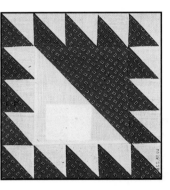

Lady of the Lake

Accession: 38.226
Original Size: 9.75"
Pattern Size: 10"
Templates:
B2   B6

Lady of the Lake

Accession: 38.679
Original Size: 14"
Pattern Size: 15"
Templates:
C3   C9

 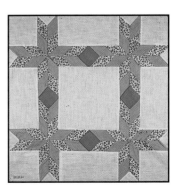

Lazy Daisy

Accession: 38.59
Original Size: 15.25"
Pattern Size: 16.25"
Templates:
A1.5   A3   A6
B1.5   E1.5   R36

Liberty Star

Accession: 38.405
Original Size: 11.75"
Pattern Size: 11"
Templates:
A1.5   R158   T61
Y2   Z2

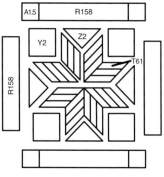

Lincoln's Platform

Accession: 38.318
Original Size: 14"
Pattern Size: 14"
Templates:
A2   B4   R26

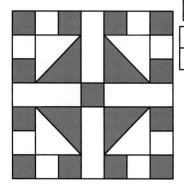

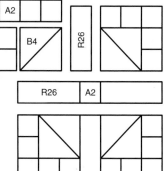

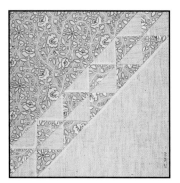

London Square

Accession: 38.21
Original Size: 10"
Pattern Size: 9"
Templates:
B1.5   B7.5

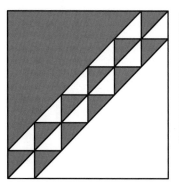

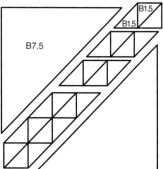

Lost Ship

Accession: 38.692
Original Size: 12"
Pattern Size: 12"
Templates:
B2   B4

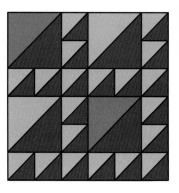

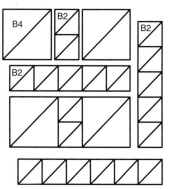

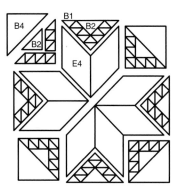

Lucinda's Star

Accession:	38.629	
Original Size:	13.5"	
Pattern Size:	13.65"	
Templates:		
B1	B2	B4
E4		

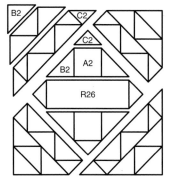

Memory Block

Accession:	38.224	
Original Size:	11.25"	
Pattern Size:	10"	
Templates:		
A2	B2	C2
R26		

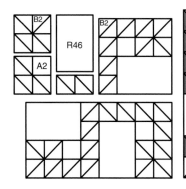

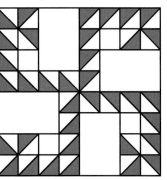

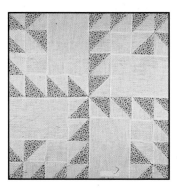

Merry Go Round
Eternal Triangle

Accession:	38.290	
Original Size:	17.5"	
Pattern Size:	16"	
Templates:		
A2	B2	R46

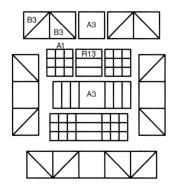

Missouri Puzzle

Accession:	38.243	
Original Size:	14.75"	
Pattern Size:	15"	
Templates:		
A1	A3	B3
R13		

Missouri Star
Shining Star

Accession: 38.627
Original Size: 16.5"
Pattern Size: 17"
Templates:
T97   X4   Y4
Z4

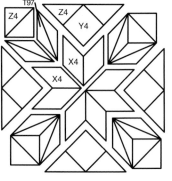

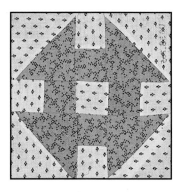

Monkey Wrench

Accession: 38.765
Original Size: 5.25"
Pattern Size: 5"
Templates:
A1   B2

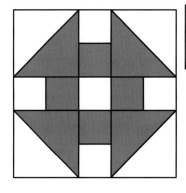

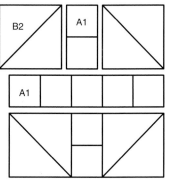

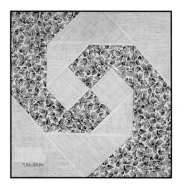

Monkey Wrench
Snail's Trail

Accession: 38.357
Original Size: 9.5"
Pattern Size: 8"
Templates:
B2   B4   C4
D2

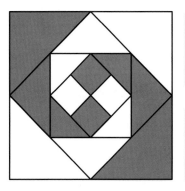

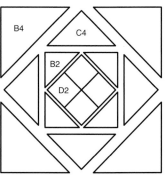

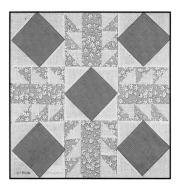

Mother's Dream

Accession: 38.111
Original Size: 11.5"
Pattern Size: 9"
Templates:
B1   B1.5   D3
R13

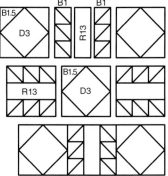

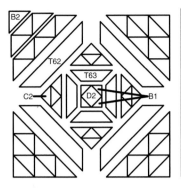

Mrs. Cleveland's Choice

County Fair

Accession:	38.316	
Original Size:	11.5"	
Pattern Size:	12"	

Templates:

B1	B2	C2
D2	T62	T63

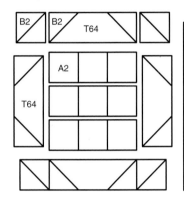

Mrs. Keller's 9 Patch

Accession:	38.194	
Original Size:	9.5"	
Pattern Size:	10"	

Templates:

A2	B2	T64

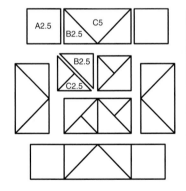

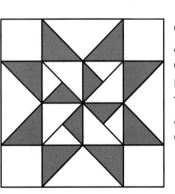

Octagonal Star

Accession:	38.795	
Original Size:	10.25"	
Pattern Size:	10"	

Templates:

A2.5	B2.5	C2.5
C5		

Octagonal Star

Dutch Rose

Accession:	38.289	
Original Size:	18.25"	
Pattern Size:	16"	

Templates:

X2	Y2	Z2

Odd Fellow's Patch

Accession: 38.304

Original Size: 14"

Pattern Size: 15"

Templates:

A3	B3	C3
C9	D6	

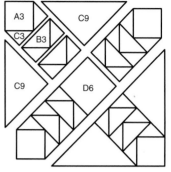

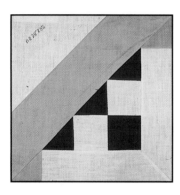

Old King Cole's Crown

Accession: 38.392

Original Size: 10"

Pattern Size: 10"

Templates:

A2	B2	B6
T66	T67	T67r

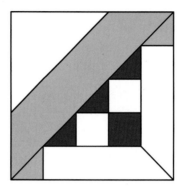

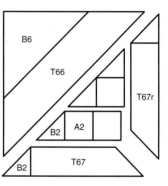

Old Maid's Puzzle

Accession: 38.150

Original Size: 9.25"

Pattern Size: 10"

Templates:

A2.5	B2.5	B5

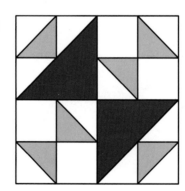

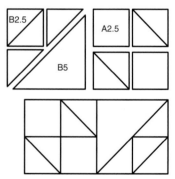

Old Maid's Ramble

Accession: 38.31

Original Size: 11.5"

Pattern Size: 12"

Templates:

C3	C6

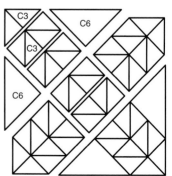

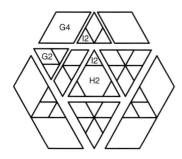

Ozark Diamond
Ozark Star
Accession: 38.284
Original Size: 13.5" x 15.75"
Pattern Size: 13.85" x 16"
Templates:
G2   G4   H2
I2

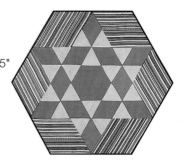

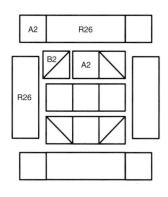
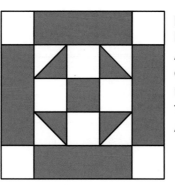

Philadelphia Pavement
Accession: 38.652
Original Size: 10"
Pattern Size: 10"
Templates:
A2   B2   R26

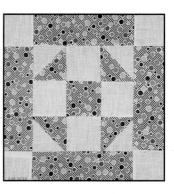

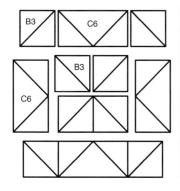
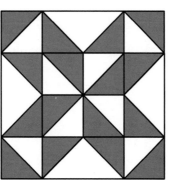

Pieced Star
Accession: 38.807
Original Size: 11.25"
Pattern Size: 12"
Templates:
B3   C6

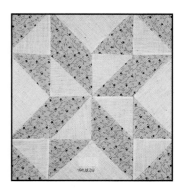

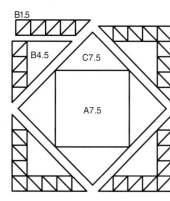

Pine Burr
Accession: 38.234
Original Size: 12.5"
Pattern Size: 15"
Templates:
A7.5   B1.5   B4.5
C7.5

Pine Tree
Temperance Tree
Accession: 38.480
Original Size: 10"
Pattern Size: 10"
Templates:
A2   B2   B6
T68   T68r   T69
T69r

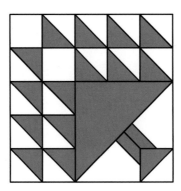

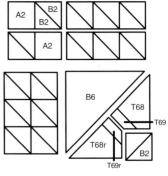

Prairie Queen
Accession: 38.693
Original Size: 9.25"
Pattern Size: 9"
Templates:
A1.5   A3   B3

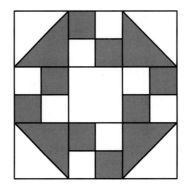

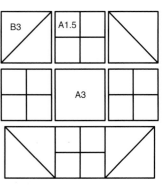

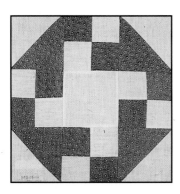

Premium Star
Accession: 38.65
Original Size: 13.75"
Pattern Size: 9"
Templates:
A1   A3   B1
R14

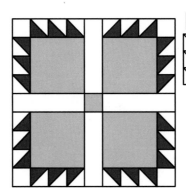

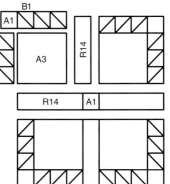

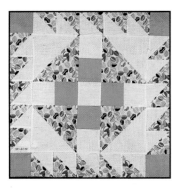

Prickly Pear
Accession: 38.172
Original Size: 15"
Pattern Size: 14"
Templates:
A2   B2   B4

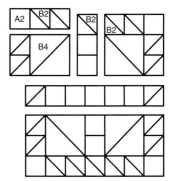

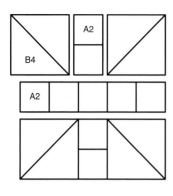
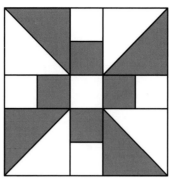

Propeller

Accession:	38.232
Original Size:	10.25"
Pattern Size:	10"
Templates:	
A2	B4

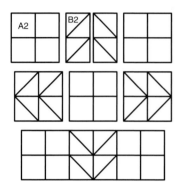
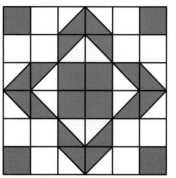
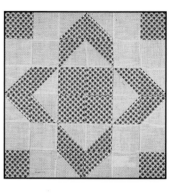

Puss-in-the-Corner
Puss'n Boots

Accession:	38.77
Original Size:	15"
Pattern Size:	12"
Templates:	
A2	B2

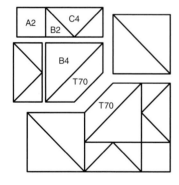
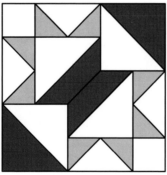
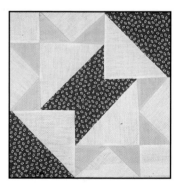

Queen Charlotte's Crown
Indian Meadow

Accession:	38.702	
Original Size:	10"	
Pattern Size:	10"	
Templates:		
A2	B2	B4
C4	T70	

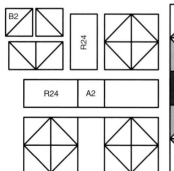
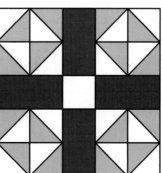

Red Cross

Accession:	38.219	
Original Size:	10.25"	
Pattern Size:	10"	
Templates:		
A2	B2	R24

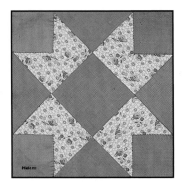

Ribbon Star

Accession: 38.159
Original Size: 11.5"
Pattern Size: 12"
Templates:

A3	B3	C6
D6		

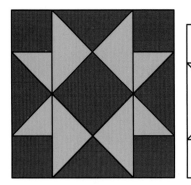
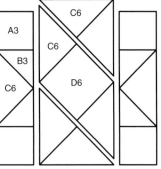

Right and Left

Accession: 38.443
Original Size: 7.25"
Pattern Size: 8"
Templates:

C4	D8

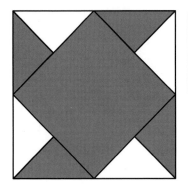
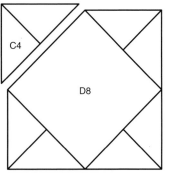

Ring Around the Star
Star and Chains

Accession: 38.174
Original Size: 14.5"
Pattern Size: 13.65"
Templates:

A2	B4	C4
E2	X3	

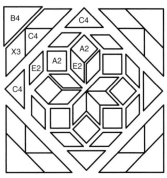

Rob Peter to Pay Paul

Accession: 38.325B
Original Size: 6"
Pattern Size: 6"
Templates:

T71	T72

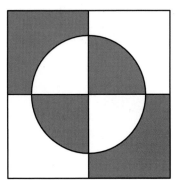
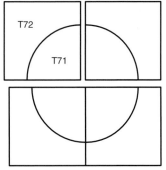

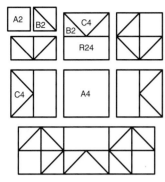

Robbing Peter to Pay Paul

Accession: 38.450
Original Size: 9.25"
Pattern Size: 12"
Templates:

A2	A4	B2
C4	R24	

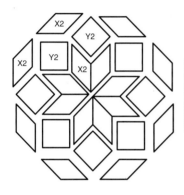
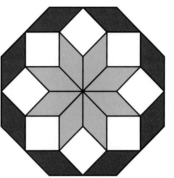

Rolling Star

Accession: 38.436
Original Size: 11"
Pattern Size: 11.28"
Templates:

X2	Y2

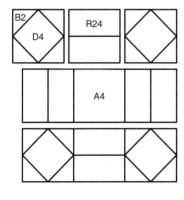
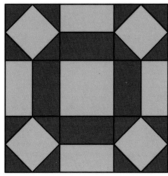

Rolling Stone
Block Circle, Johnnie Round the Corner

Accession: 38.612
Original Size: 9.25"
Pattern Size: 12"
Templates:

A4	B2	D4
R24		

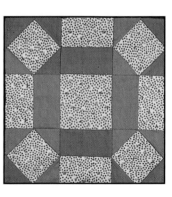

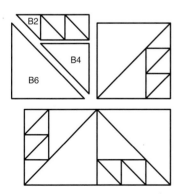
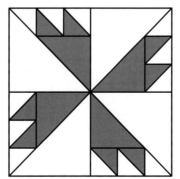

Rosebud

Accession: 38.363
Original Size: 11.75"
Pattern Size: 12"
Templates:

B2	B4	B6

Royal Star

Accession: 38.162

Original Size: 12.5"

Pattern Size: 12"

Templates:

C4	D4	T73
T74	T74r	

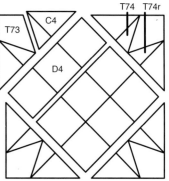

Sage Bud

Accession: 38.71

Original Size: 14.25"

Pattern Size: 12"

Templates:

A2	A4	B2
C2	T75	T75r

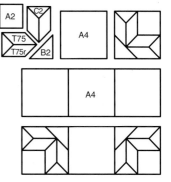

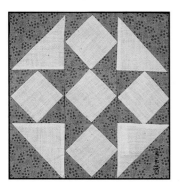

Sawtooth

Accession: 38.123

Original Size: 7.75"

Pattern Size: 9"

Templates:

B1.5	B3	D3

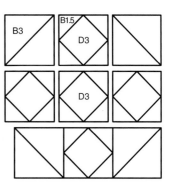

Scotch Plaid

Accession: 38.139

Original Size: 8.75"

Pattern Size: 8"

Templates:

B2	C2	D4
F1		

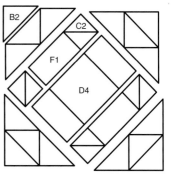

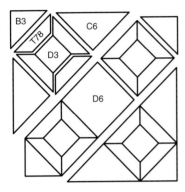

Secret Drawer
Spools

Accession: 38.127

Original Size: 12"

Pattern Size: 12"

Templates:

B3	C6	D3
D6	T78	

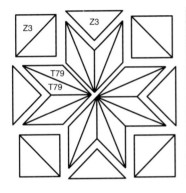

Silver and Gold
Star of the East

Accession: 38.412

Original Size: 10"

Pattern Size: 10"

Templates:

T79	Z3

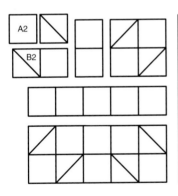

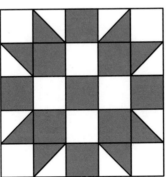

Sister's Choice

Accession: 38.381

Original Size: 10"

Pattern Size: 10"

Templates:

A2	B2

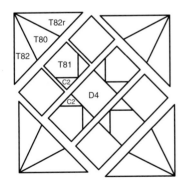

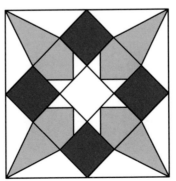

Sky Rocket

Accession: 38.148

Original Size: 11.75"

Pattern Size: 12"

Templates:

C2	D4	T80
T81	T82	T82r

Snow Crystals

Accession: 38.185

Original Size: 15"

Pattern Size: 16"

Templates:

T31   X2   Y2
Z2

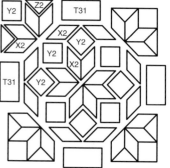

Solomon's Temple

Accession: 38.327

Original Size: 15.25"

Pattern Size: 15"

Templates:

A1.5   A4.5   B1.5
B4.5   C7.5

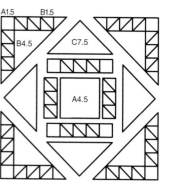

Spinning Triangles

Accession: 38.102

Original Size: 15.25"

Pattern Size: 15"

Template: T83

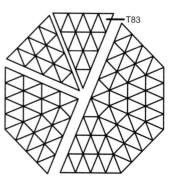

Spinning Wheel
Pin Wheel

Accession: 38.633

Original Size: 13"

Pattern Size: 12"

Templates:

A4   B2   B4
D2

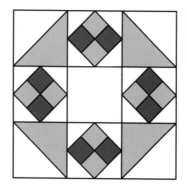

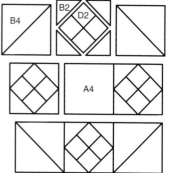

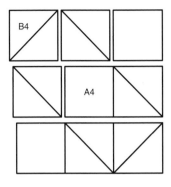
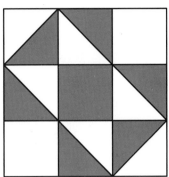

Split 9 Patch

Accession: 38.130

Original Size: 12"

Pattern Size: 12"

Templates:

A4   B4

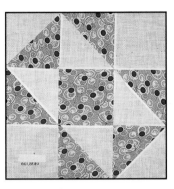

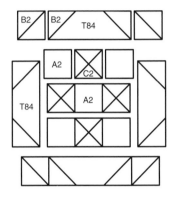

Square and a Half

Accession: 38.86

Original Size: 9.5"

Pattern Size: 10"

Templates:

A2   B2   C2

T84

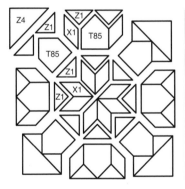

Star of Bethlehem

Accession: 38.623

Original Size: 12.25"

Pattern Size: 12"

Templates:

T85   X1   Z1

Z4

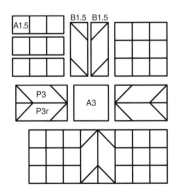

Stepping Stones

Accession: 38.147

Original Size: 12"

Pattern Size: 12"

Templates:

A1.5   A3   B1.5

P3   P3r

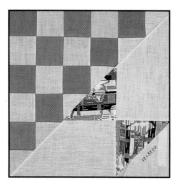

Steps to the Altar

Accession: 38.151

Original Size: 10.5"

Pattern Size: 12"

Templates:

A2	B2	B4
T86	T86r	

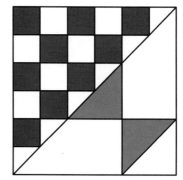

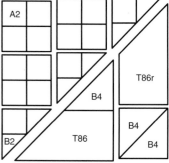

Swallows in the Window

Accession: 38.180

Original Size: 8.5"

Pattern Size: 8"

Templates:

A4	C4	X0
Y0	Z0	

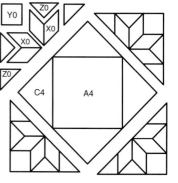

Swing in the Center

Accession: 38.230

Original Size: 13"

Pattern Size: 12"

Templates:

B2	C4	D4
T90		

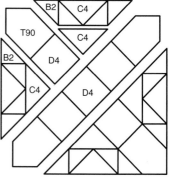

Toad-in-a-Puddle

Accession: 38.119

Original Size: 12"

Pattern Size: 12"

Templates:

B3	C3	C6
D6		

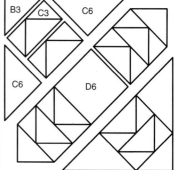

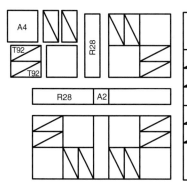

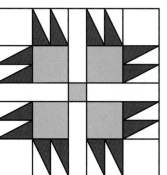

Turkey Tracks

Accession: 38.779
Original Size: 18.5"
Pattern Size: 18"
Templates:
A2   A4   T92
R28

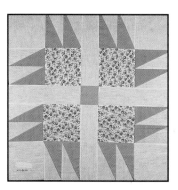

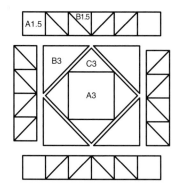

Union Square

Accession: 38.140
Original Size: 9.5"
Pattern Size: 9"
Templates:
A1.5   A3   B1.5
B3   C3

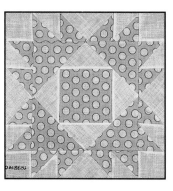

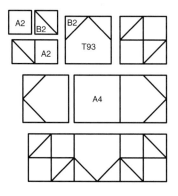

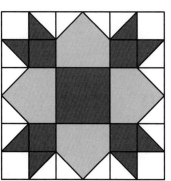

Weathervane

Accession: 38.158
Original Size: 12"
Pattern Size: 12"
Templates:
A2   A4   B2
T93

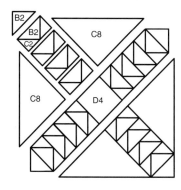

Wild Goose Chase

Accession: 38.182
Original Size: 12.5"
Pattern Size: 12"
Templates:
B2   C2   C8
D4

Wind-blown Star

Accession: 38.89
Original Size: 9.5"
Pattern Size: 10"
Templates:
B2.5   C5   D5

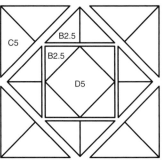

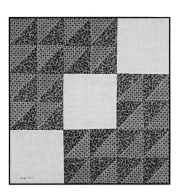

Winged Square

Accession: 38.690
Original Size: 12"
Pattern Size: 12"
Templates:
A4   B2

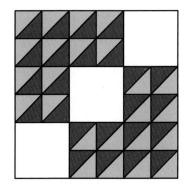

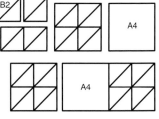

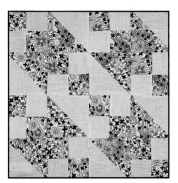

World's Fair

Accession: 38.630
Original Size: 12.5"
Pattern Size: 12"
Templates:
A1.5   B3

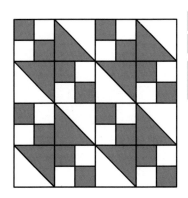

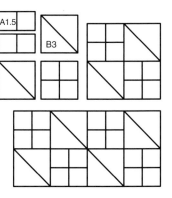

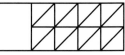

Yankee Pride

Accession: 38.722
Original Size: 12"
Pattern Size: 12"
Templates:
X1   Y1   Z1

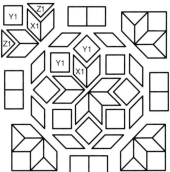

Template Patterns

Template Patterns

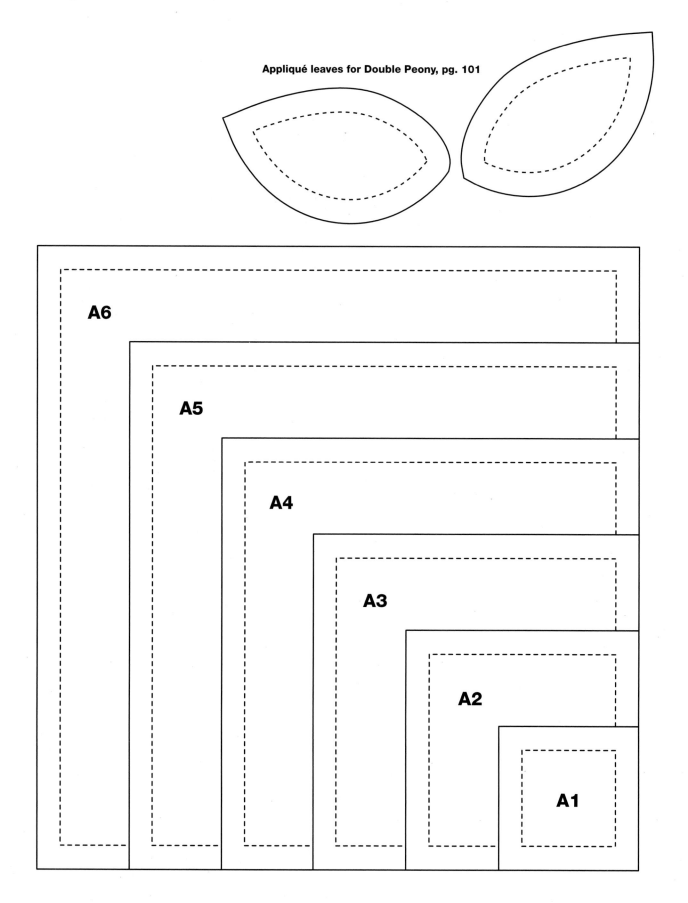

Appliqué leaves for Double Peony, pg. 101

A6

A5

A4

A3

A2

A1

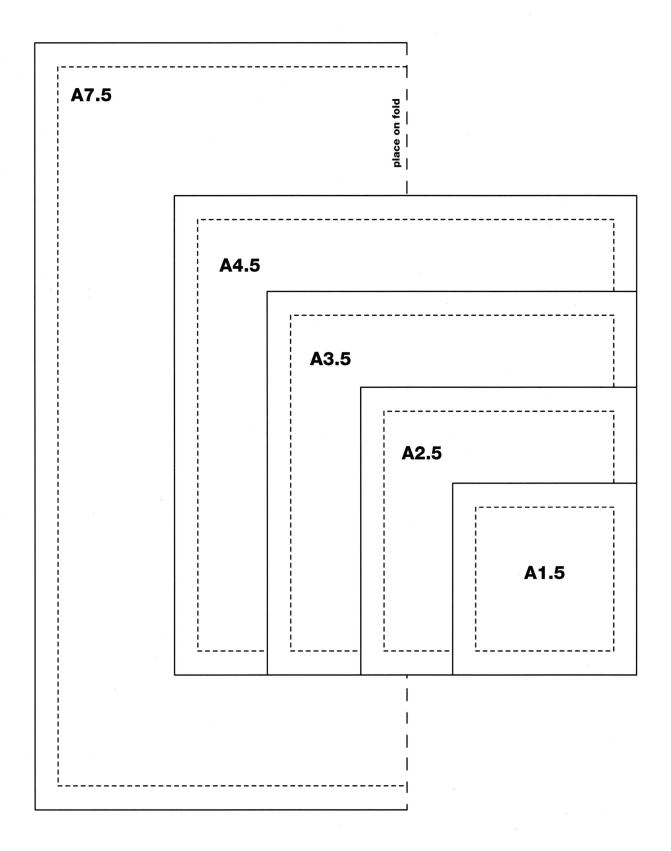

A7.5

place on fold

A4.5

A3.5

A2.5

A1.5

Template Patterns

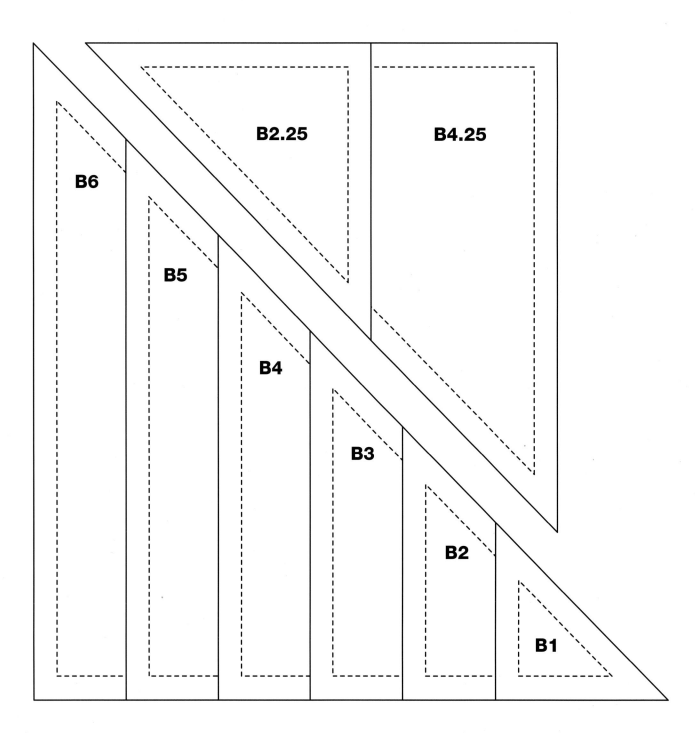

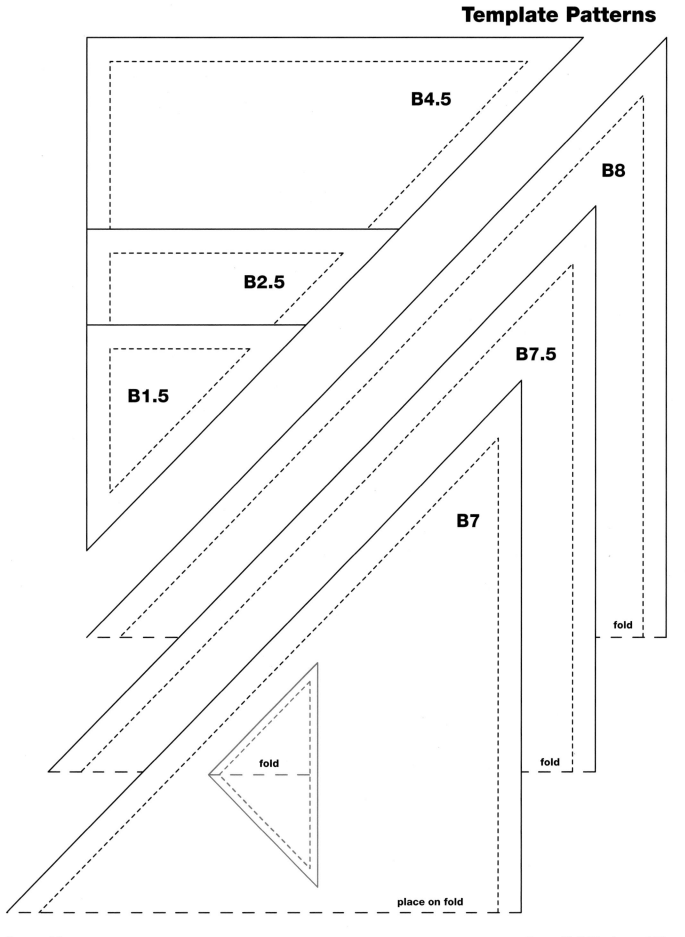

B4.5

B8

B2.5

B7.5

B1.5

B7

fold

fold

fold

place on fold

Template Patterns

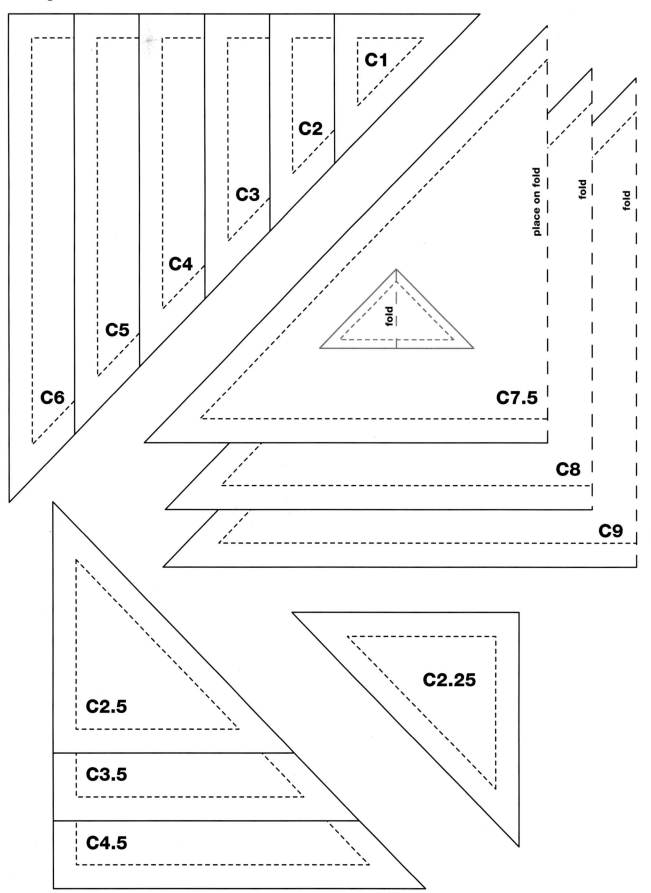

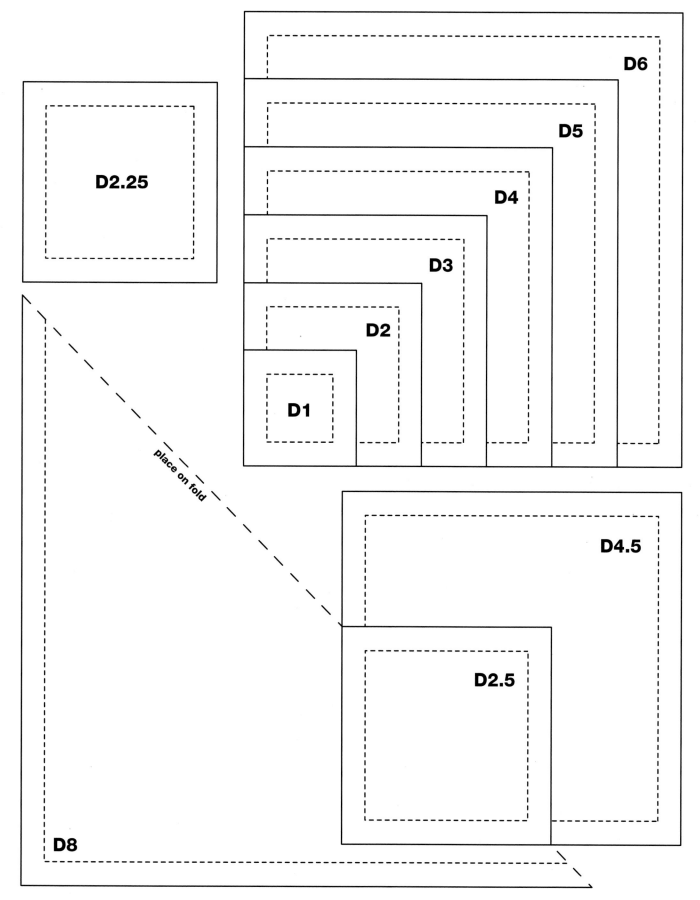

Template Patterns

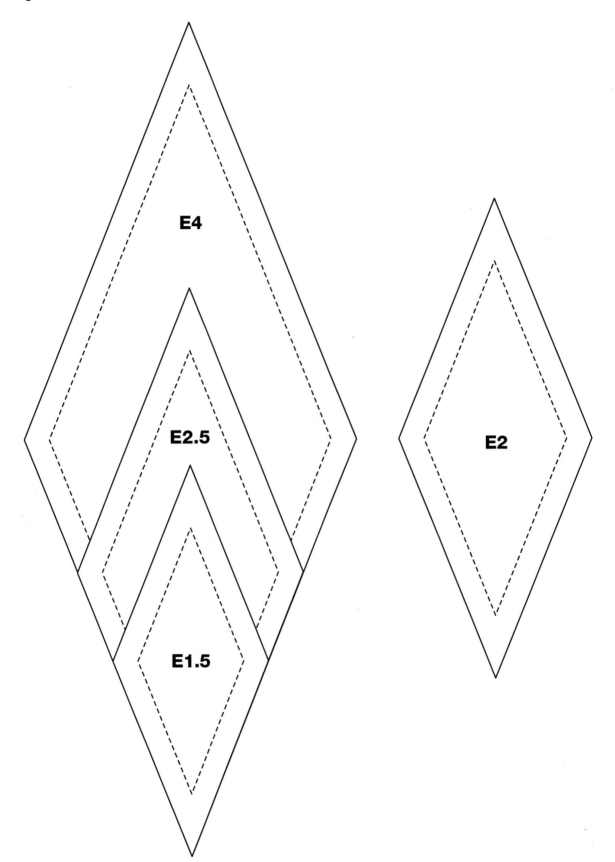

E4

E2.5

E1.5

E2

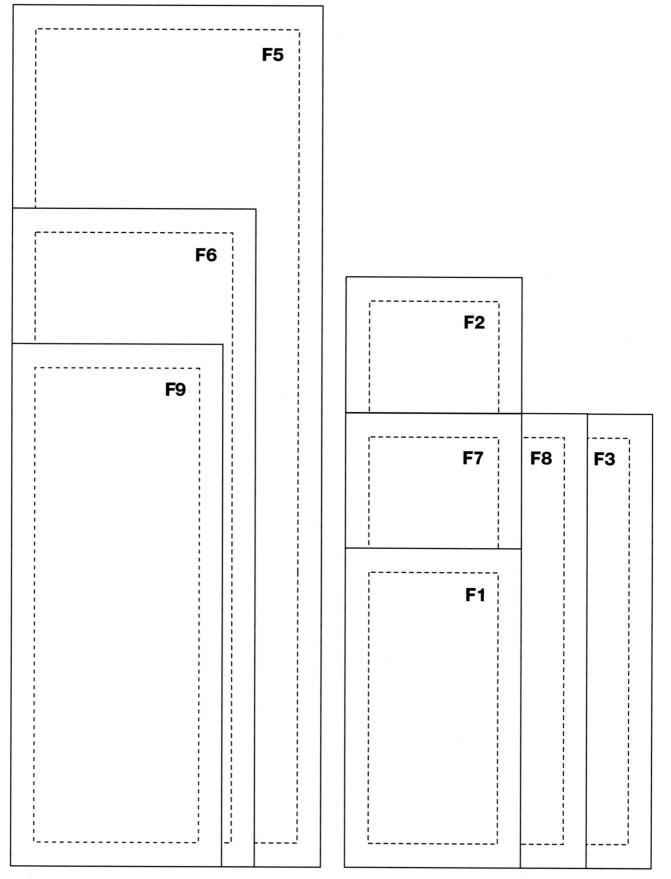

F5

F6

F9

F2

F7 F8 F3

F1

Template Patterns

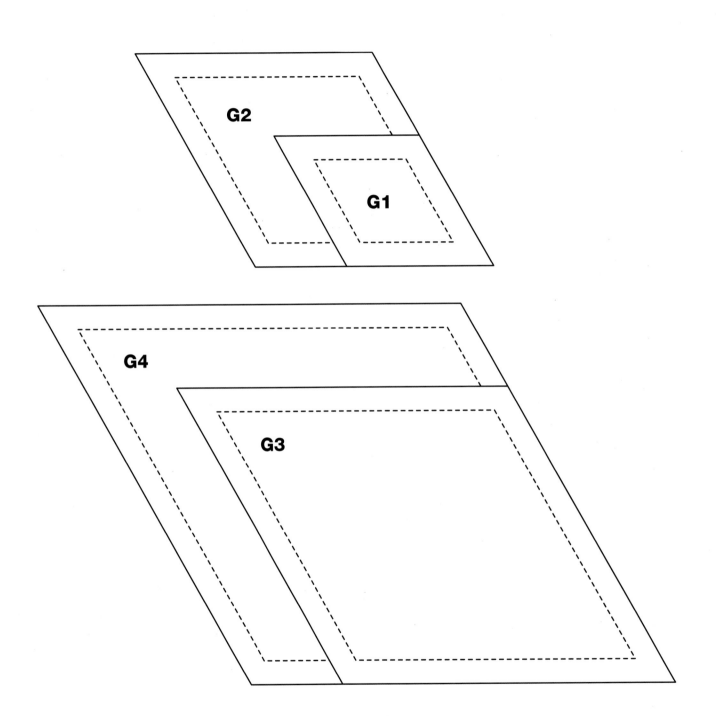

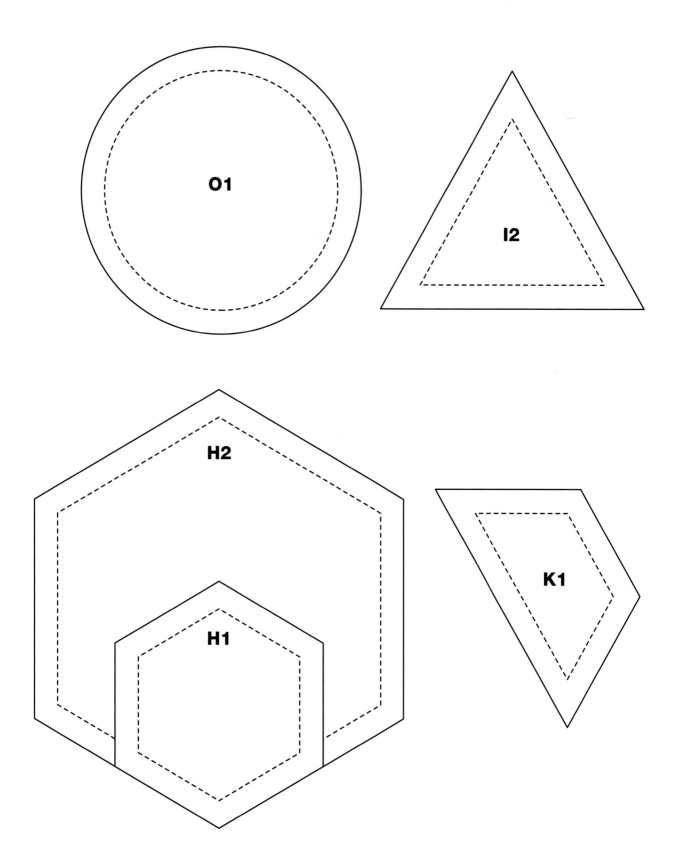

O1

I2

H2

H1

K1

Template Patterns

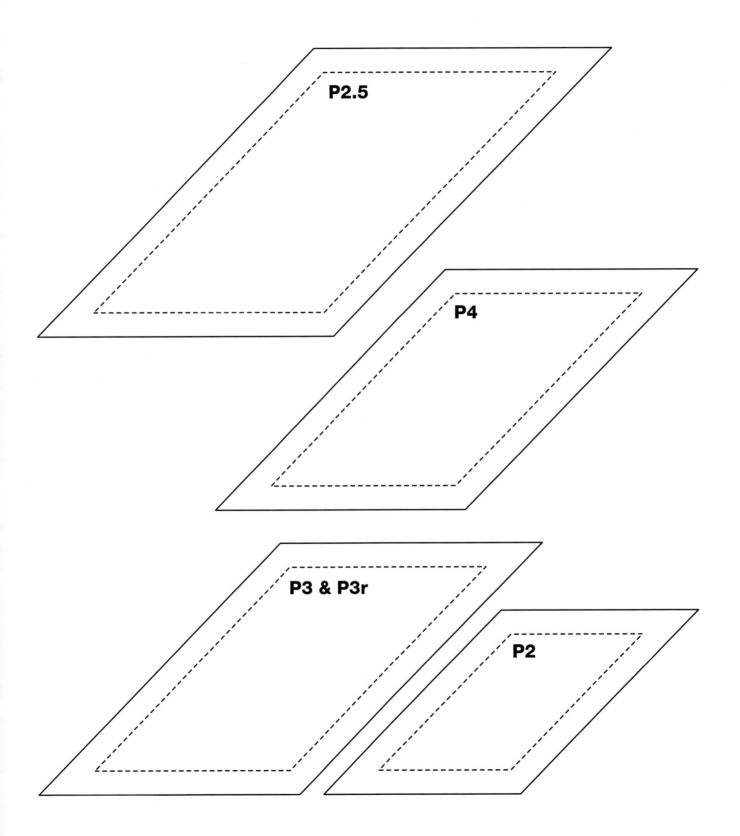

P2.5

P4

P3 & P3r

P2

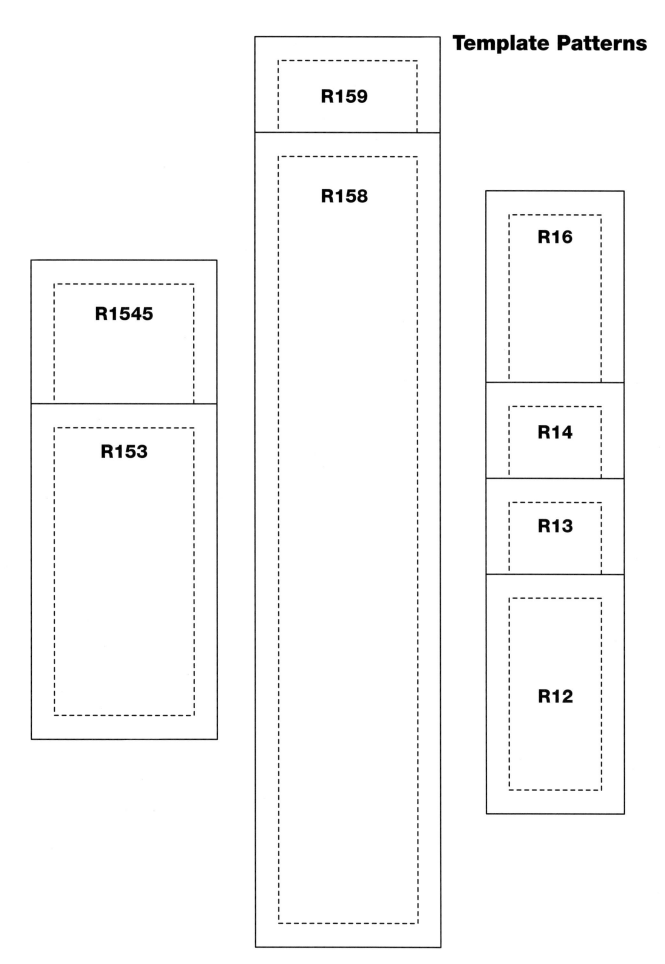

R159

R158

R1545

R153

R16

R14

R13

R12

Template Patterns

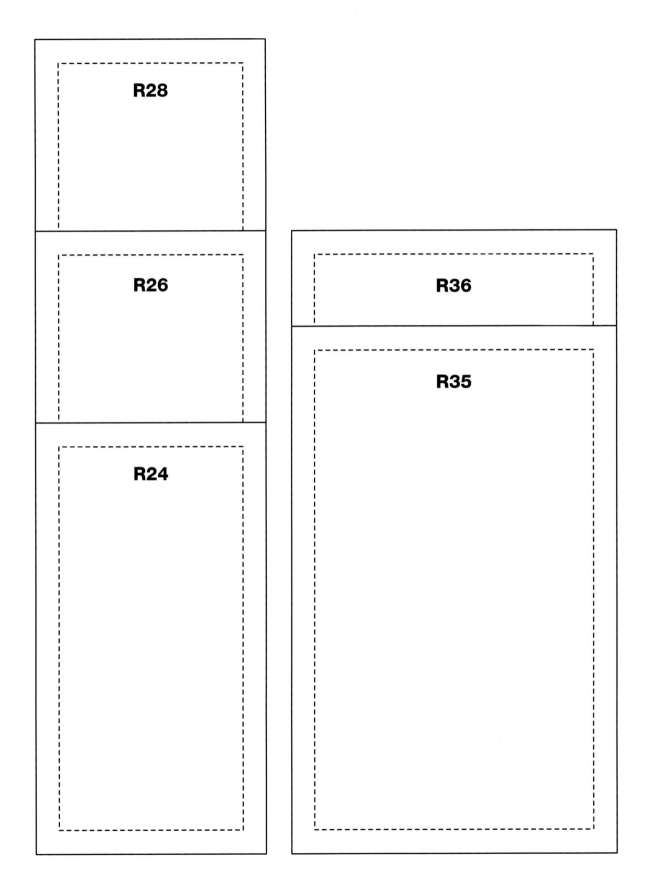

R28

R26

R24

R36

R35

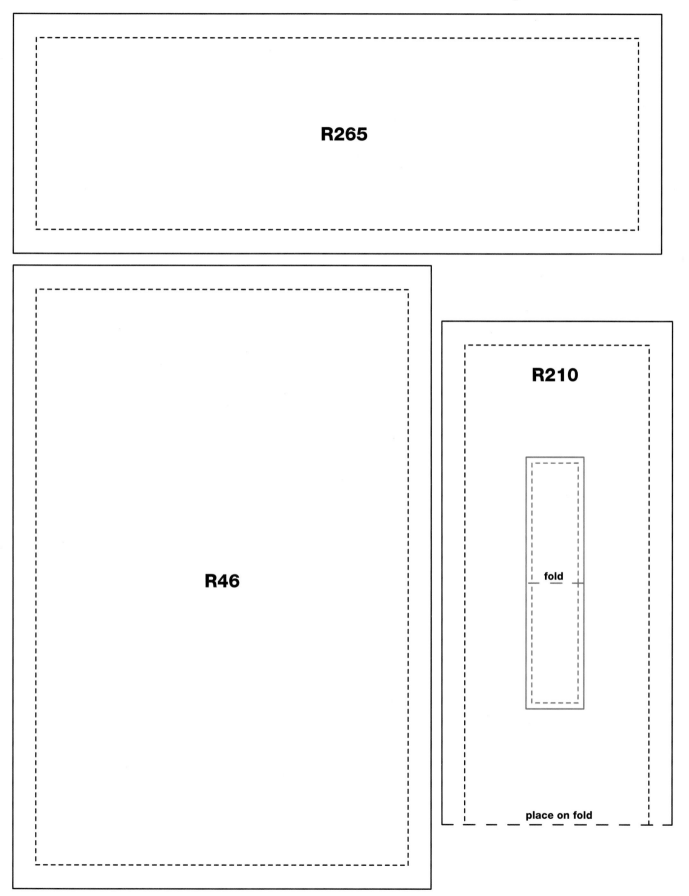

R265

R46

R210

fold

place on fold

Template Patterns

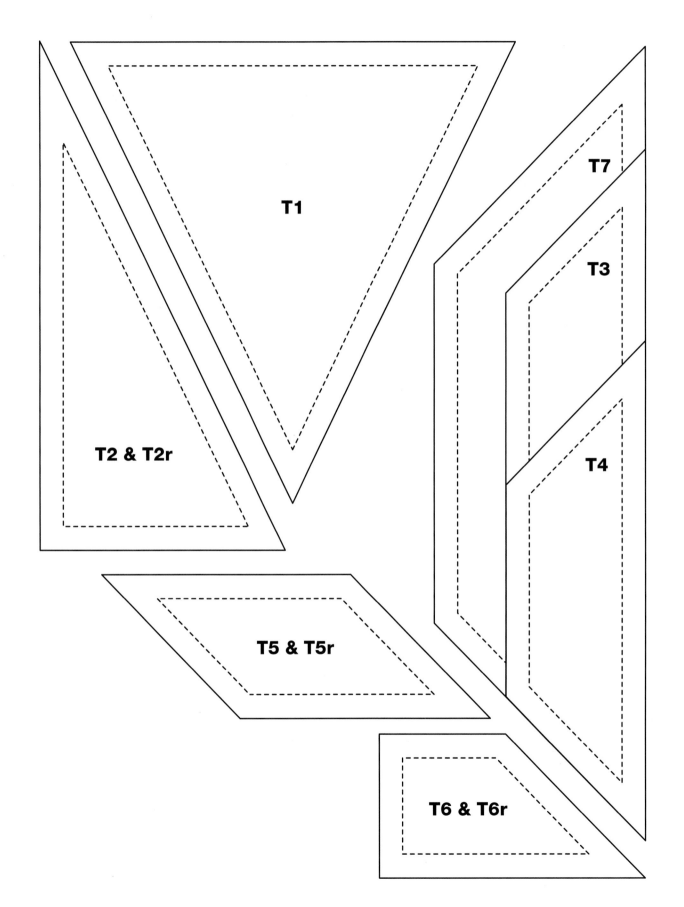

T1

T2 & T2r

T7

T3

T4

T5 & T5r

T6 & T6r

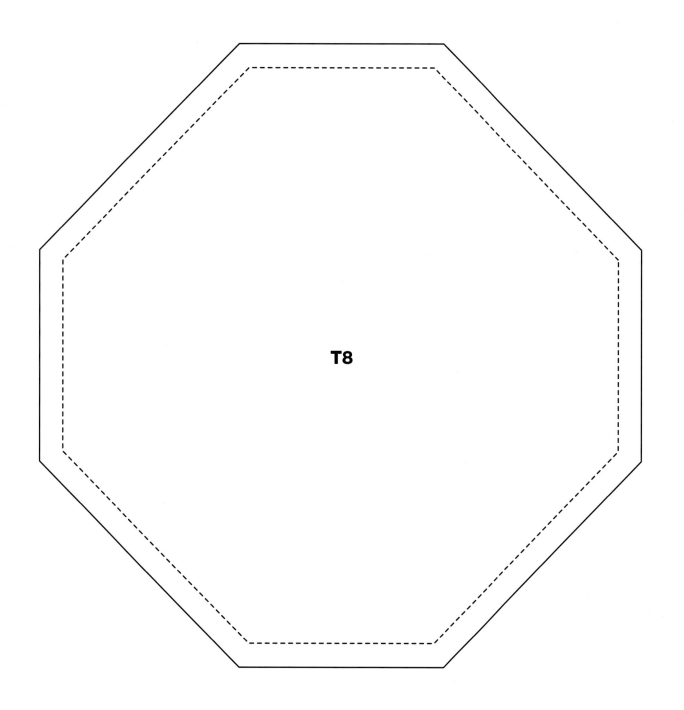

T8

Template Patterns

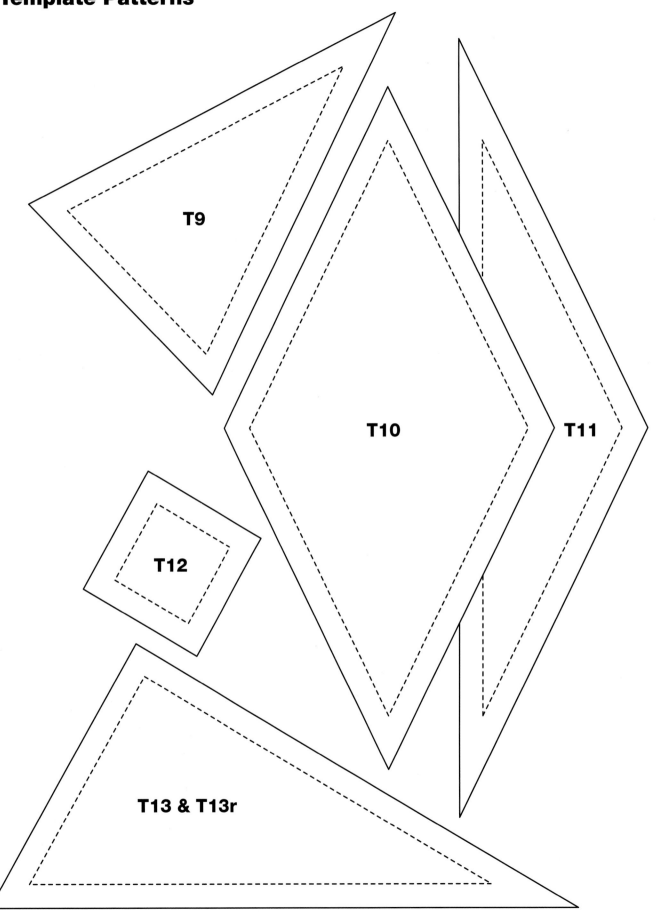

T9

T10

T11

T12

T13 & T13r

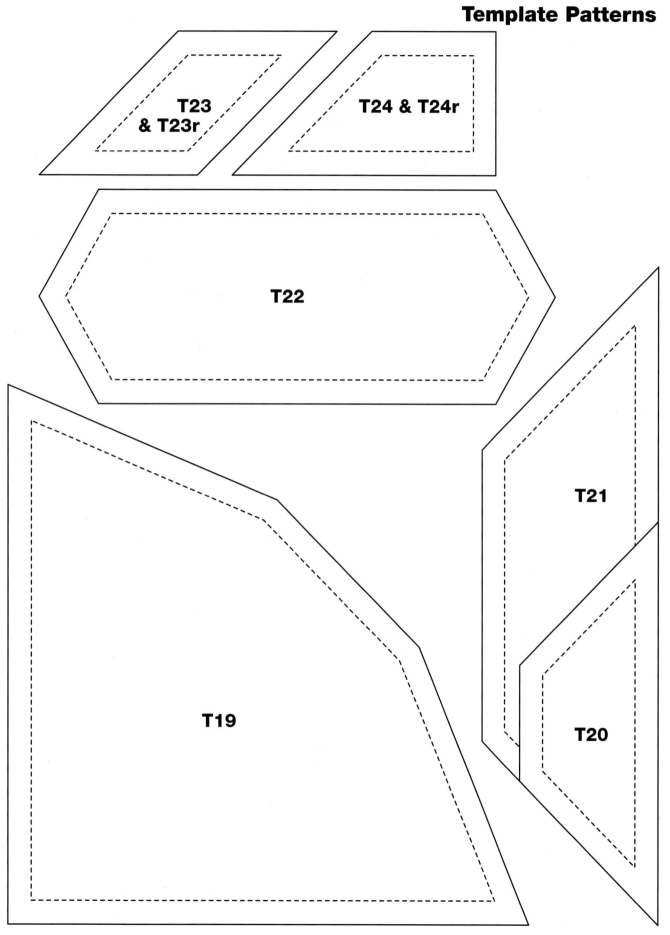

T23
& T23r

T24 & T24r

T22

T21

T19

T20

Template Patterns

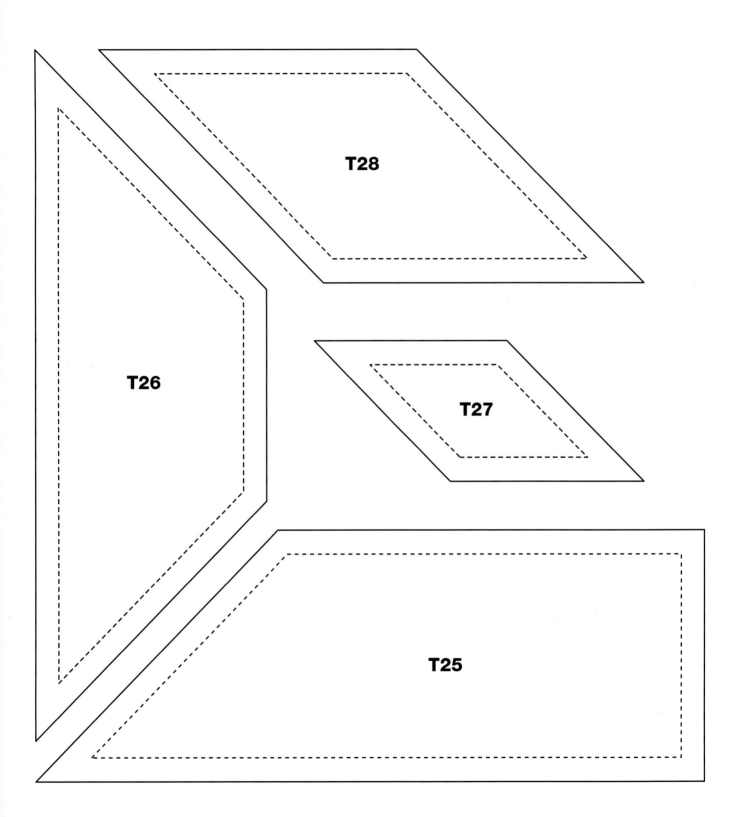

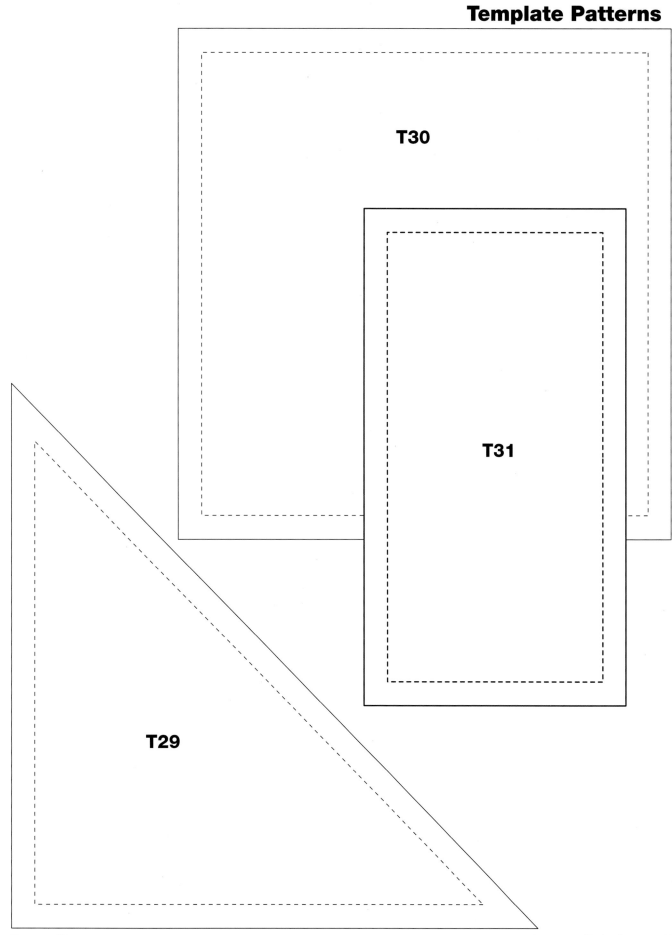

T30

T31

T29

Template Patterns

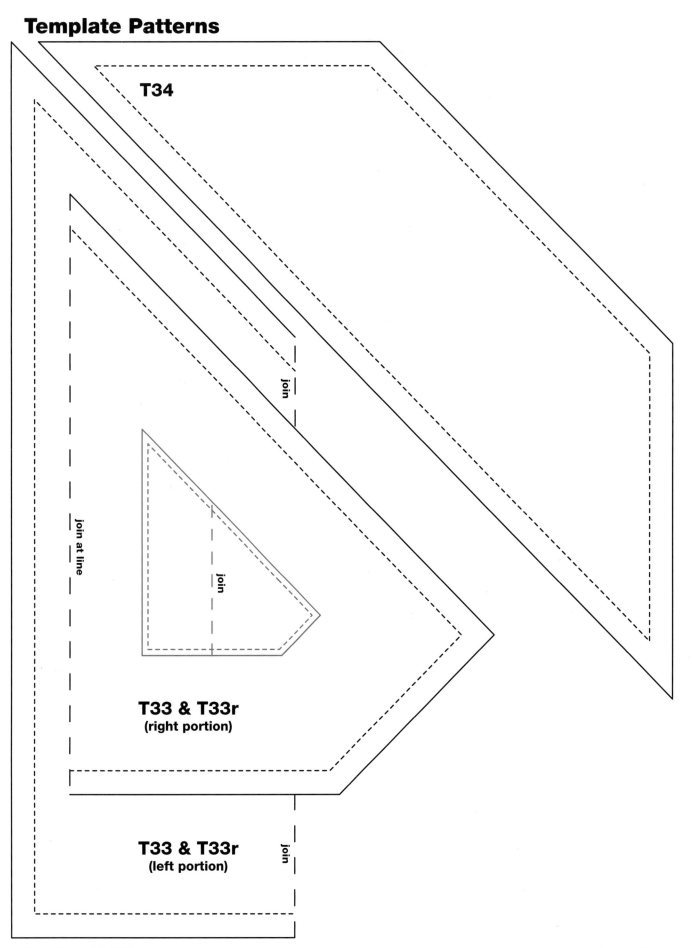

T34

join

join at line

join

T33 & T33r
(right portion)

T33 & T33r
(left portion)

join

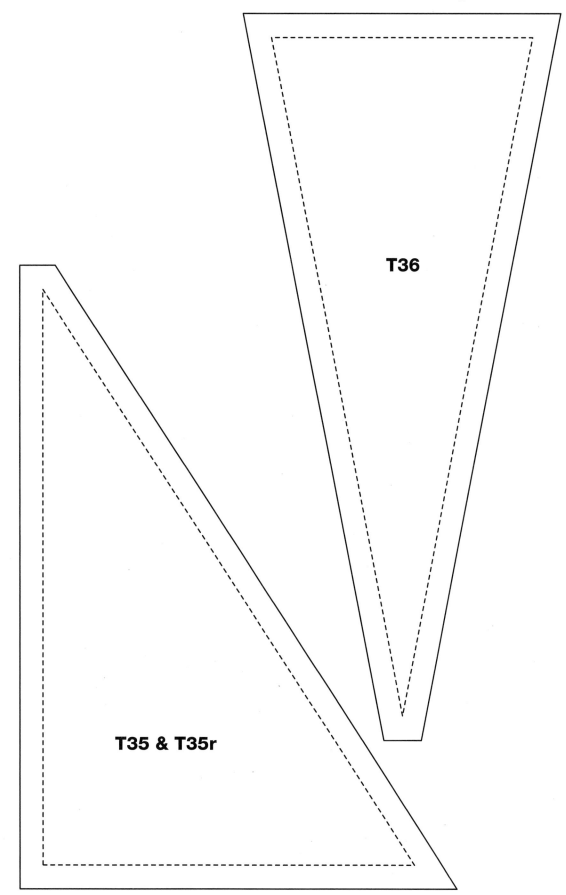

T36

T35 & T35r

Template Patterns

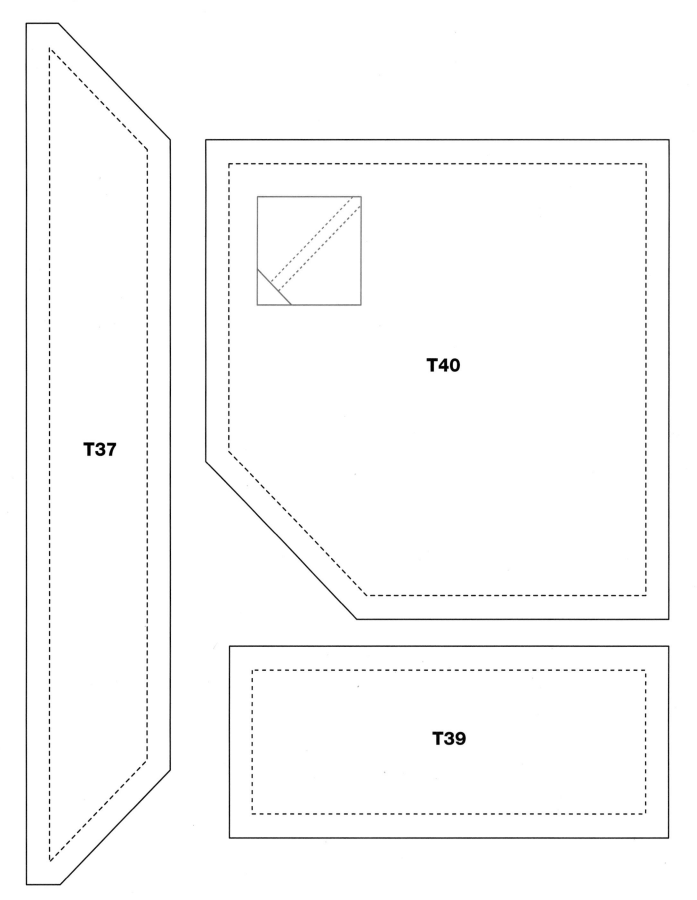

T37

T40

T39

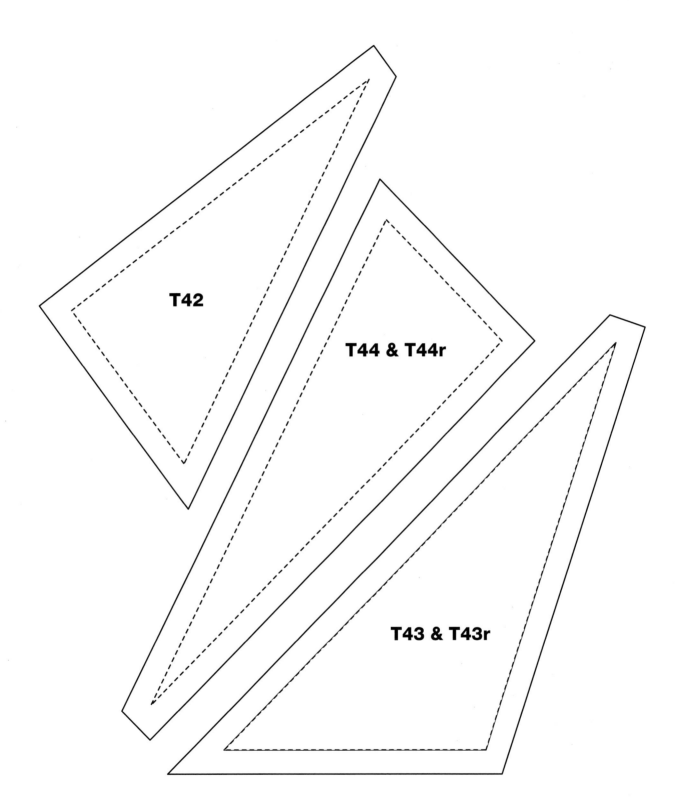

T42

T44 & T44r

T43 & T43r

Template Patterns

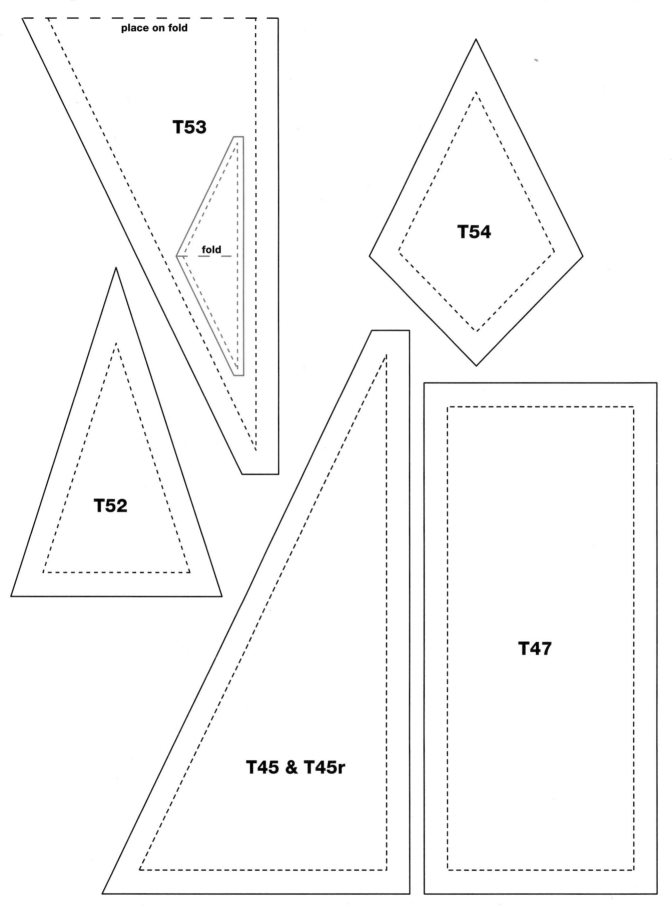

place on fold

T53

fold

T54

T52

T45 & T45r

T47

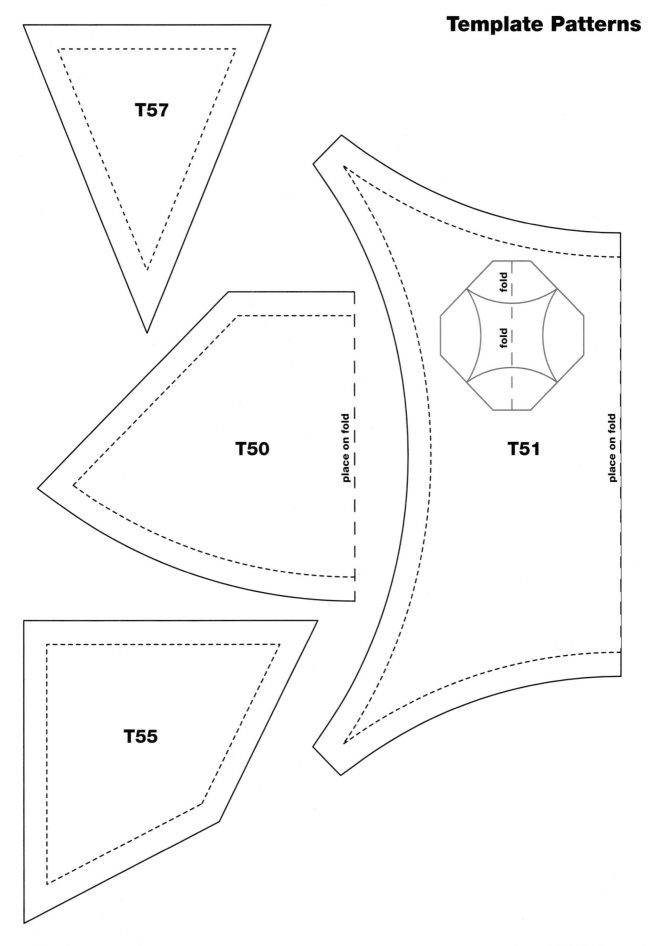

T57

T50

place on fold

T51

place on fold

fold

fold

fold

T55

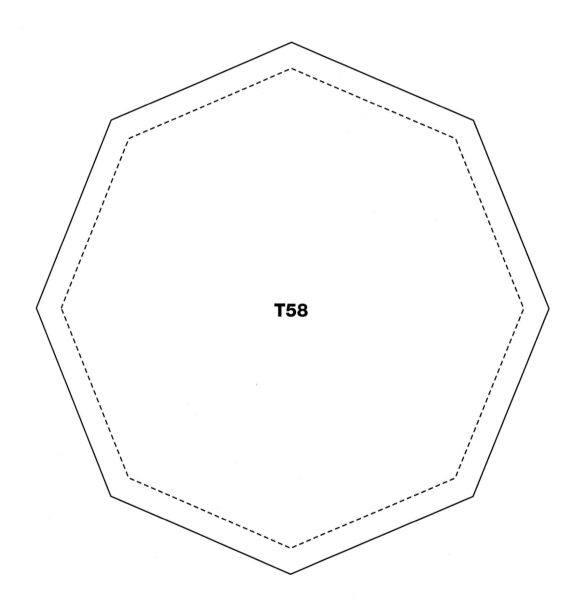

T58

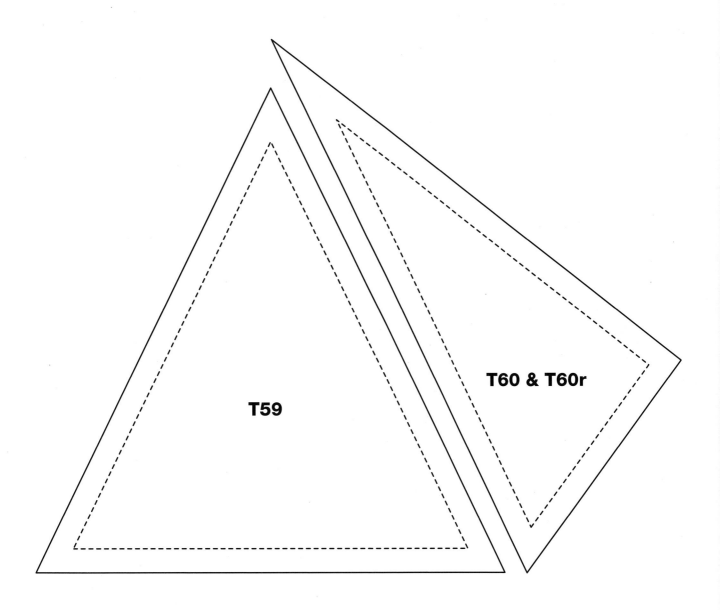

T59

T60 & T60r

Template Patterns

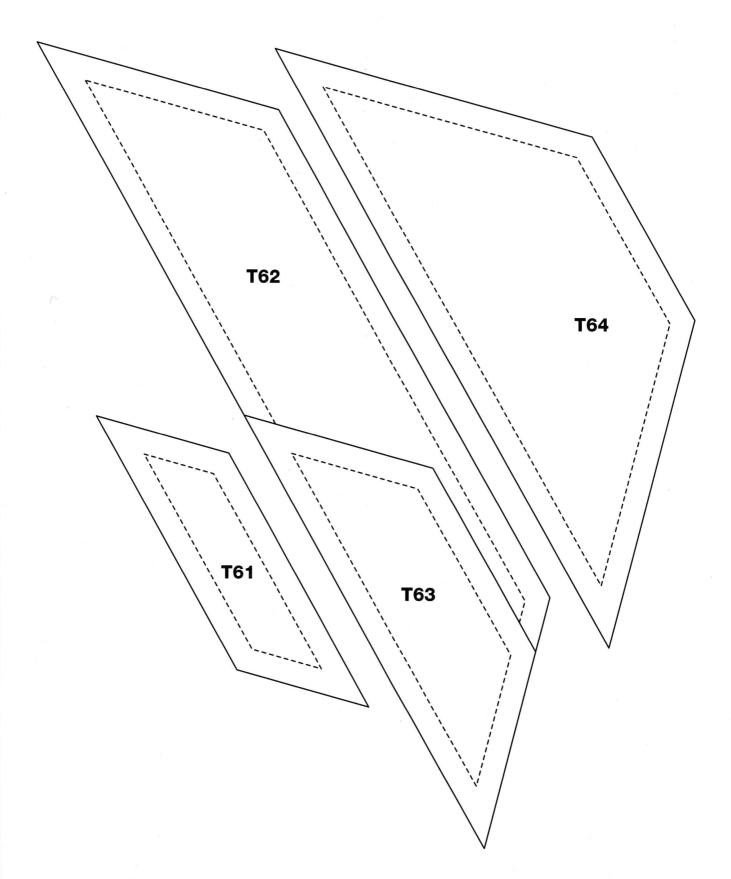

T62

T64

T61

T63

Bettina Havig

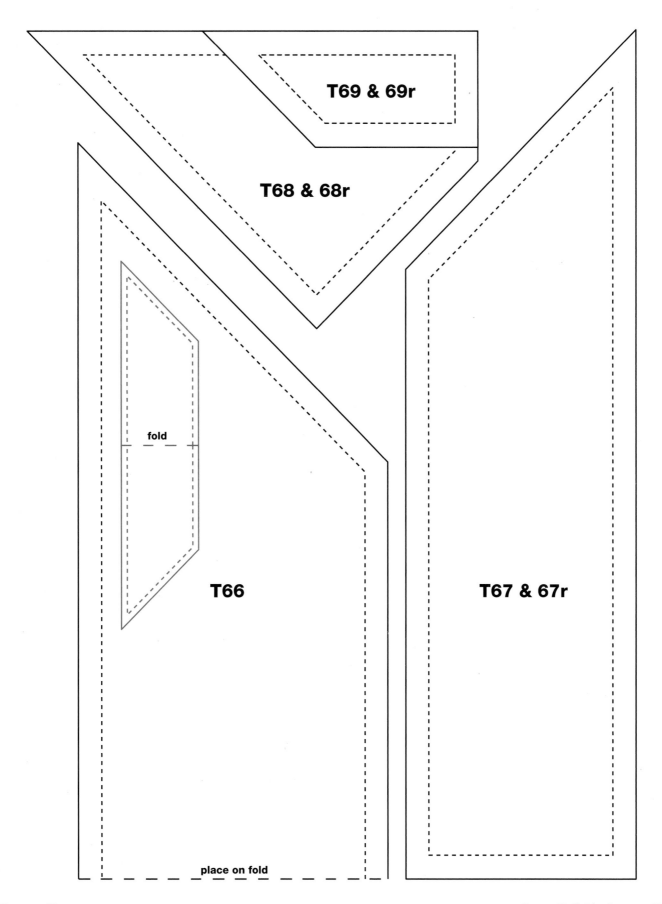

T69 & 69r

T68 & 68r

fold

T66

T67 & 67r

place on fold

Template Patterns

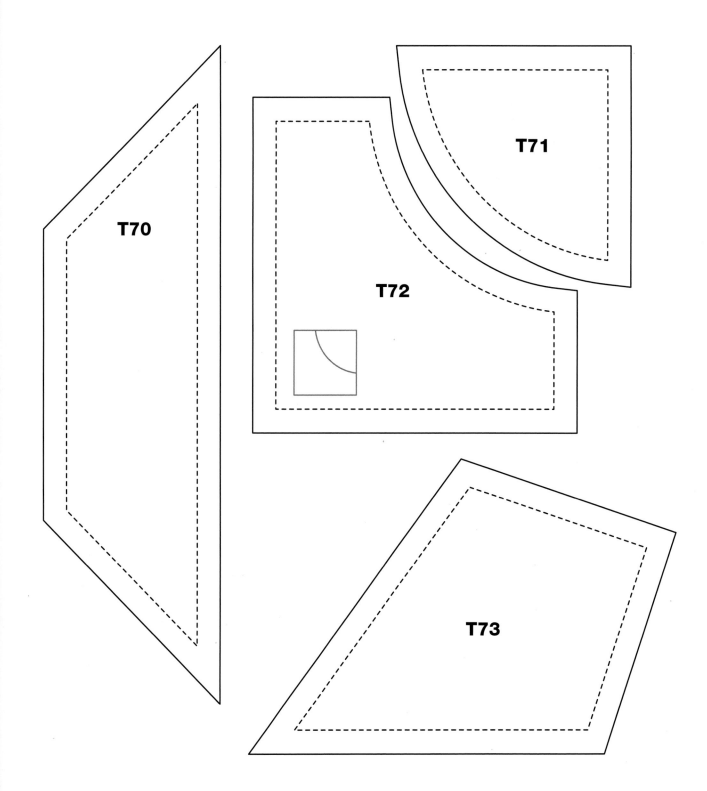

T70

T71

T72

T73

Bettina Havig

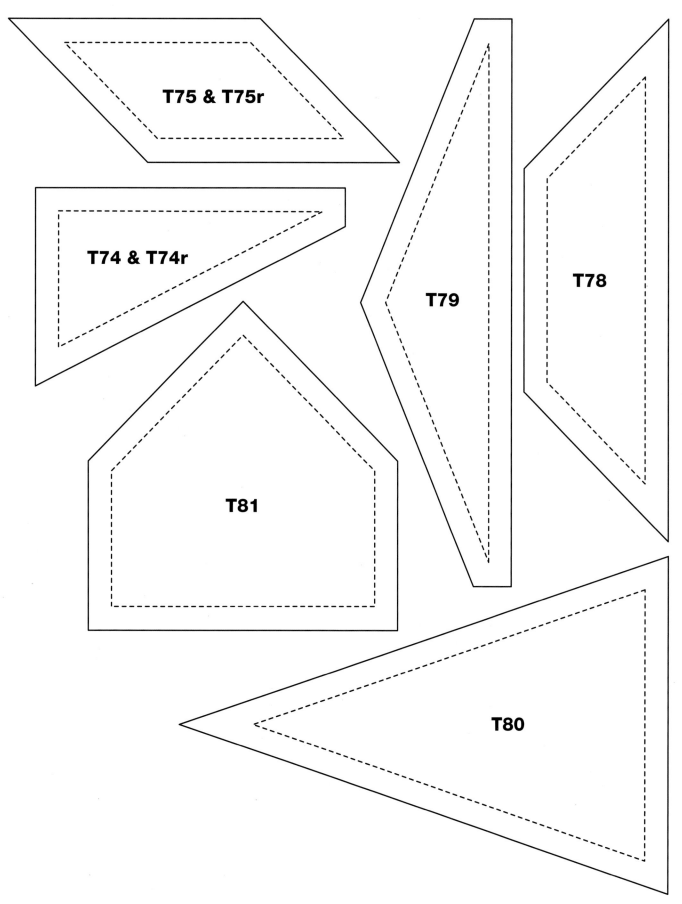

T75 & T75r

T74 & T74r

T79

T78

T81

T80

Template Patterns

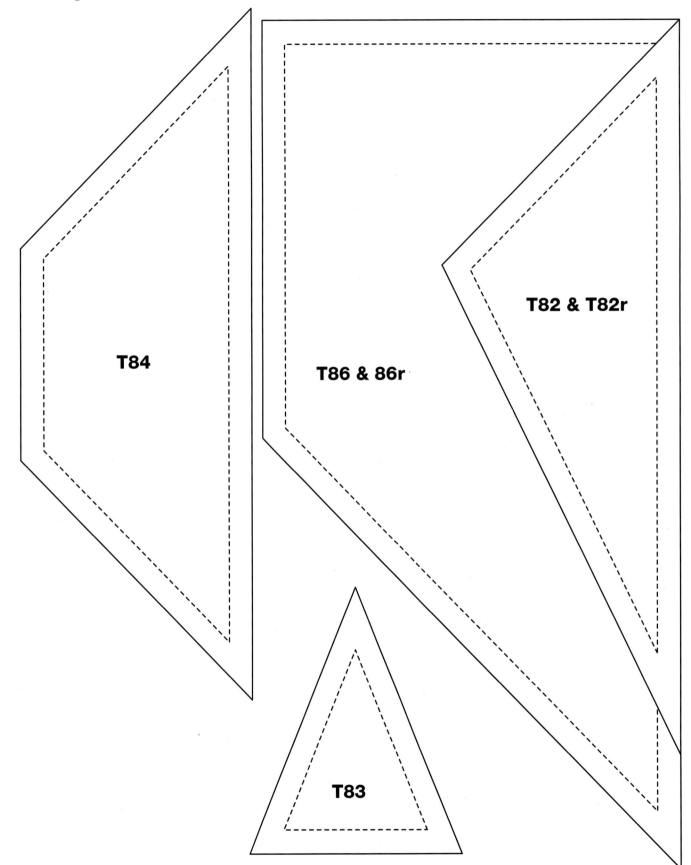

T84

T86 & 86r

T82 & T82r

T83

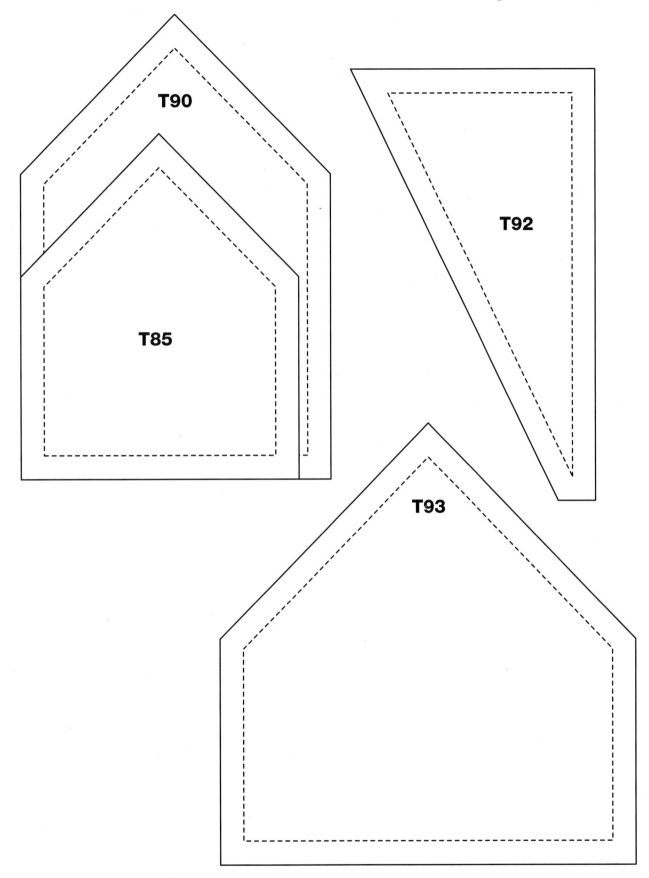

T90

T85

T92

T93

Template Patterns

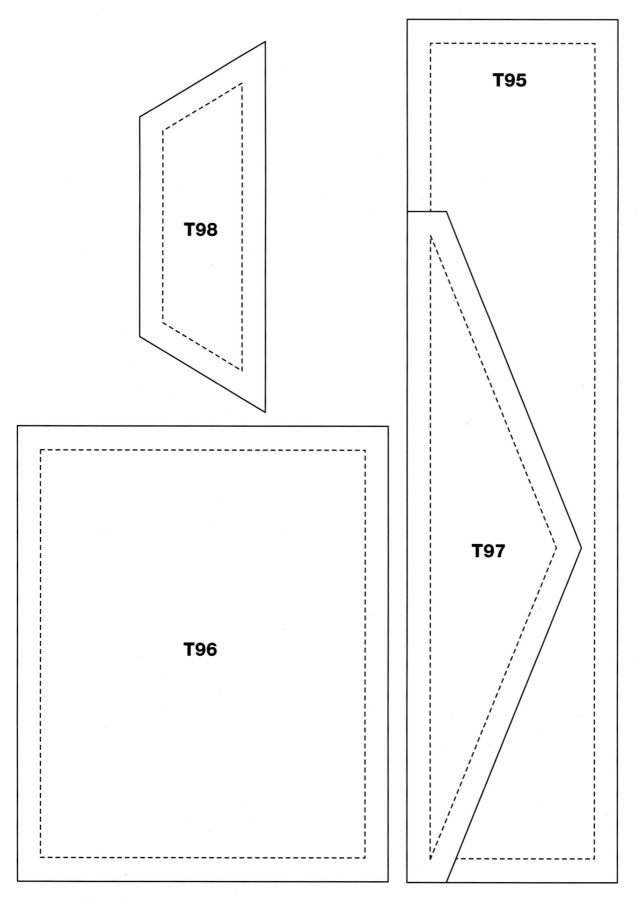

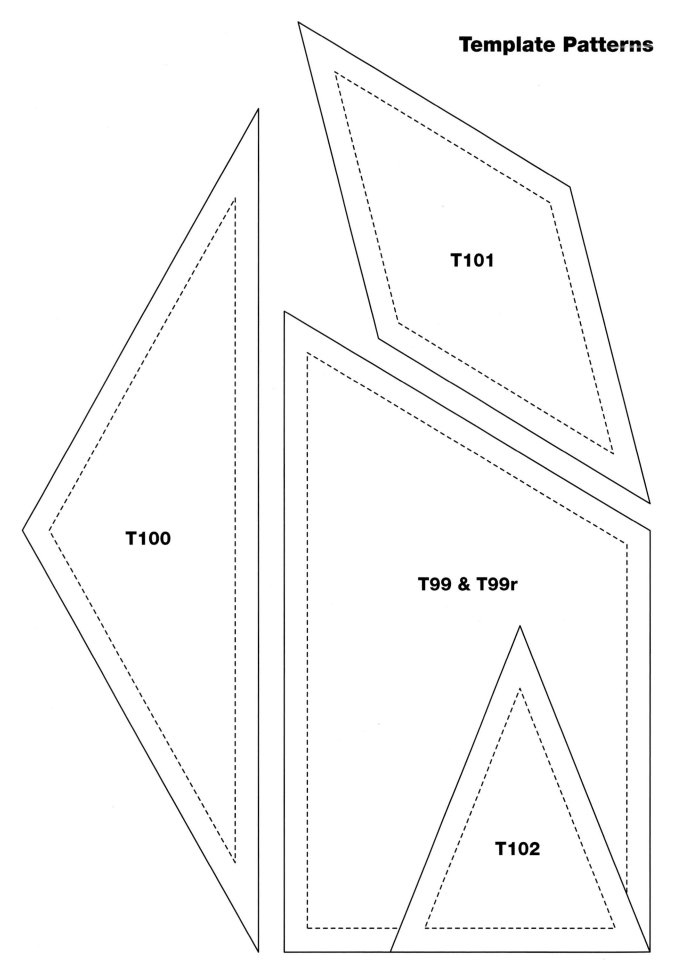

T101

T100

T99 & T99r

T102

Template Patterns

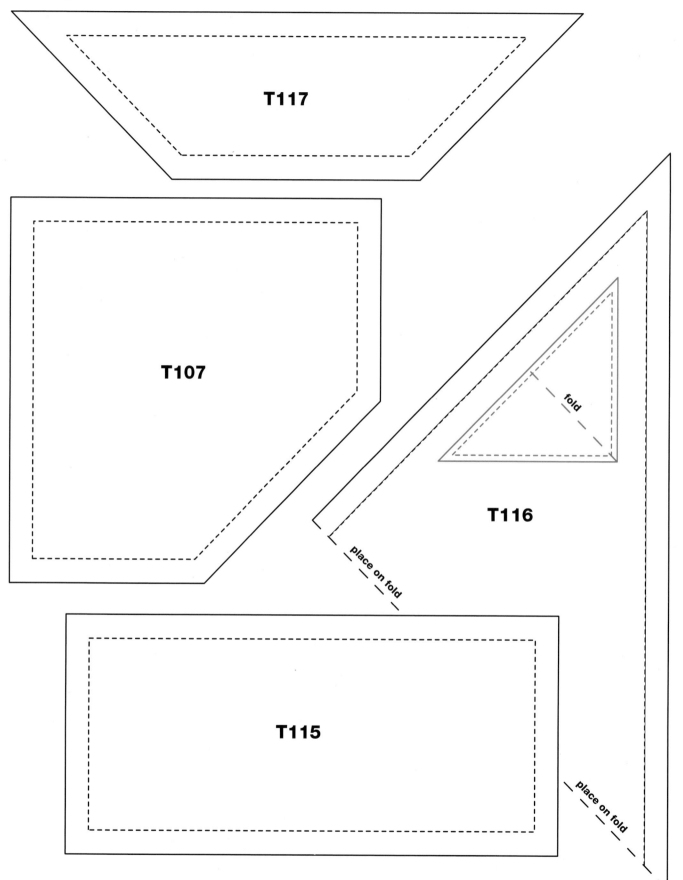

T117

T107

T116

fold

place on fold

T115

place on fold

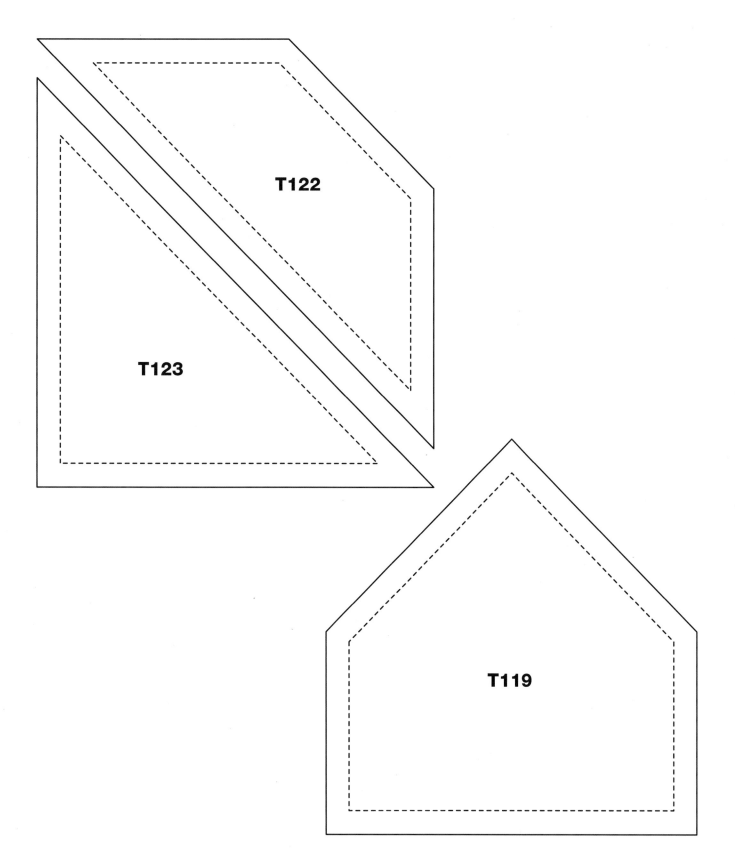

T122

T123

T119

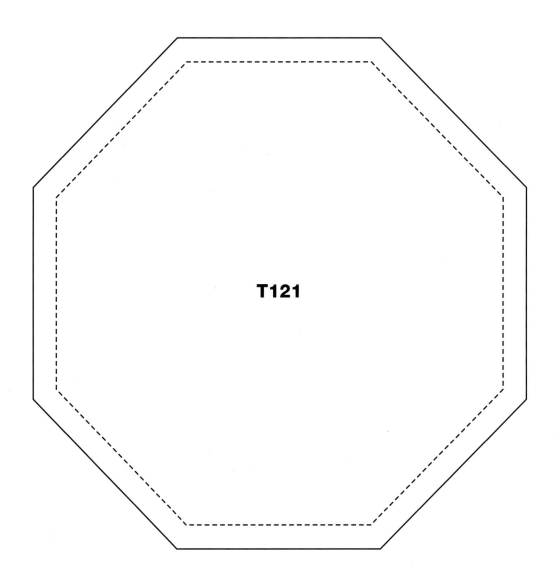

T121

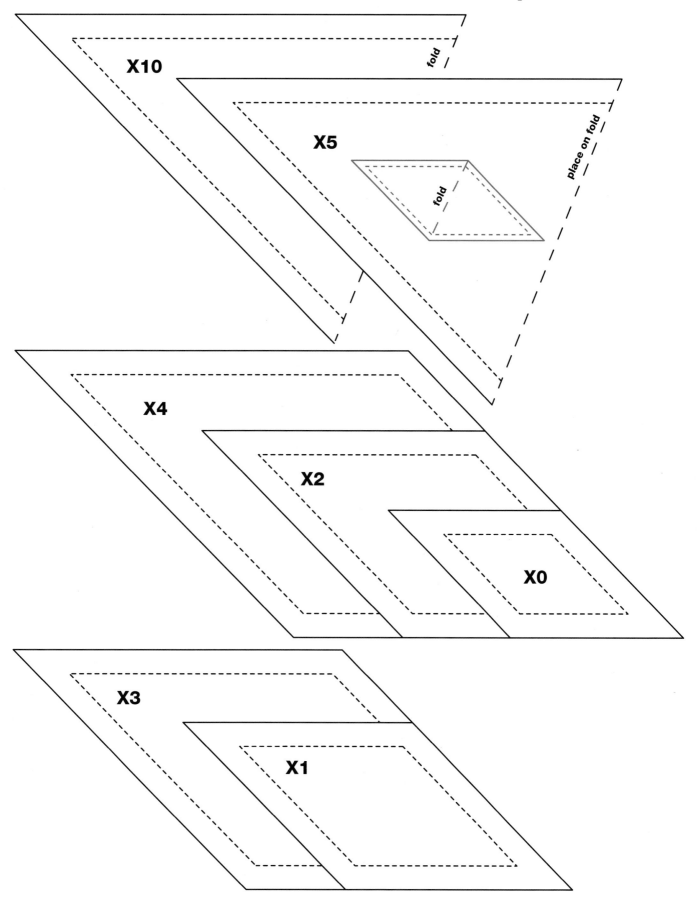

X10

fold

X5

place on fold

fold

X4

X2

X0

X3

X1

Template Patterns

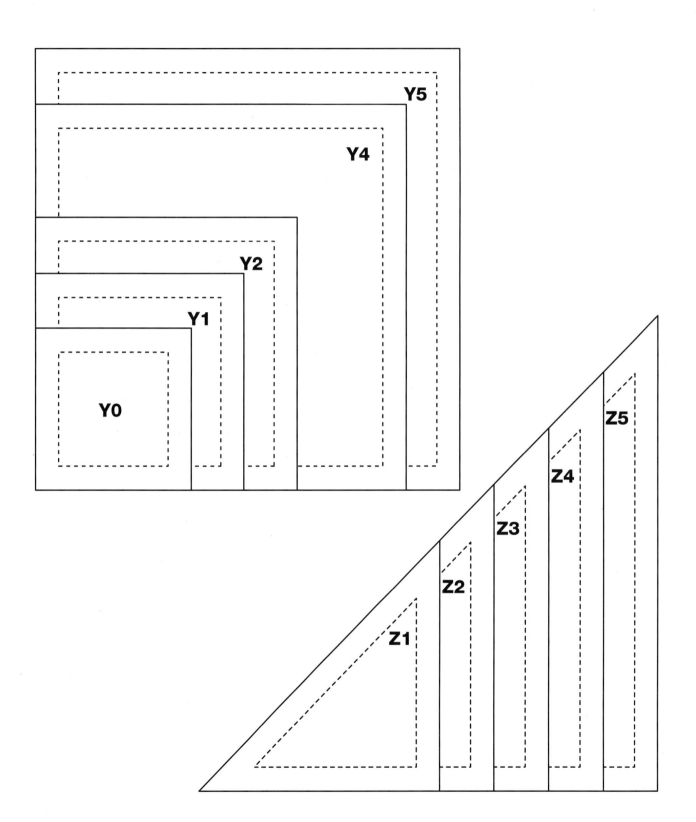

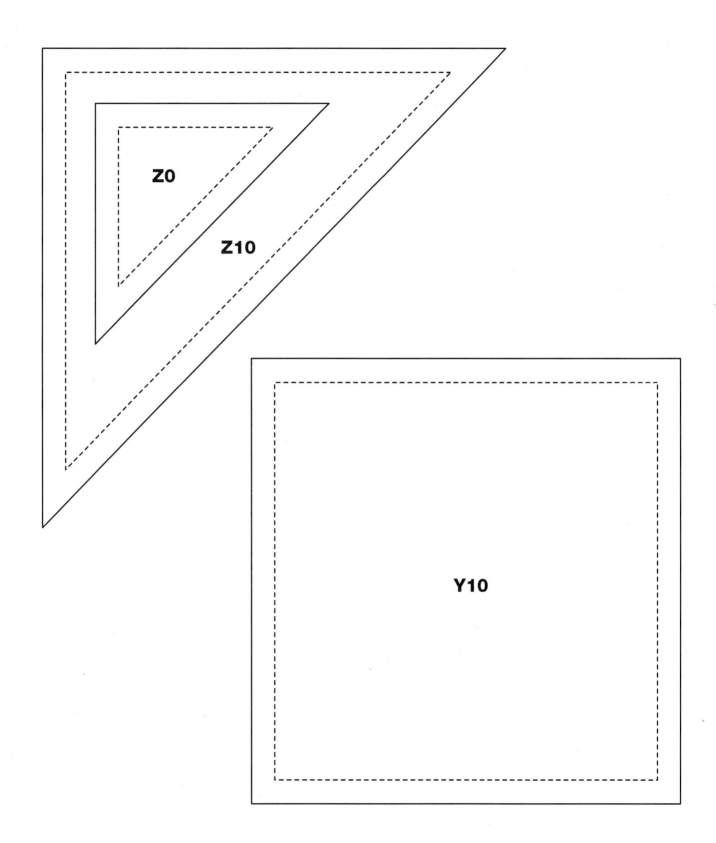

Z0

Z10

Y10

Index

Index

Index

AQS Books on Quilts

This is only a partial listing of the books available from the American Quilter's Society. AQS books are known worldwide for timely topics, clear writing, beautiful color photos, and accurate illustrations and patterns. The following books are available from your local bookseller, quilt shop, or public library. If you are unable to locate certain titles in your area, you may order by mail from the AMERICAN QUILTER'S SOCIETY, P.O. Box 3290, Paducah, KY 42002-3290. Add $2.00 for postage for the first book ordered and 40¢ for each additional book. Include item number, title, and price when ordering. Allow 14 to 21 days for delivery. Customers with Visa, MasterCard, or Discover may phone in orders from 7:00–5:00 CST, Mon.–Fri., 1-800-626-5420.